CAREERS IN COMPUTING AND INFORMATION TECHNOLOGY

David Yardley

KOGAN PAGE

First published in 1997

Kogan Page Limited
120 Pentonville Road
London N1 9JN

© Kogan Page, 1997

British Library Cataloguing in Publication Data

A CIP record for this book is available from the British Library.

ISBN 0 7494 2432 X

Typeset by Northern Phototypesetting Co Ltd, Bolton
Printed and bound in Great Britain by Clays Ltd, St Ives plc

for Anne

Contents

support; Freelance IT contractors; Occupations outside
the IT department

Acknowledgements

I would like to take this opportunity to thank the many individuals and organisations who offered information and advice during the early stages of the book's development. For Tables 2.1 and 2.2, I must express my gratitude to *Computer Weekly*, for kind permission to reproduce their employment statics.

In particular, I would like to thank the following organisations for sparing the time and effort in answering the torrent of questions I had prepared for them:

IBM UK
Intel Ireland Ltd
Oracle UK
Cap Gemini UK
Tertio Limited
Case Technology
The Post Office
EMAP Construct

Finally, I would like to thank Anne Browning, not only for her help in the preparation of the manuscript but also for her patience and encouragement throughout the project.

1 Introduction

☐ Do you have an interest in computers, the way in which they can be used or the benefits they can bring?

☐ Are you keen to join an industry which is one of the fastest growing in the world?

☐ Do you want to be in well-paid and relatively secure employment?

☐ Are you prepared to change jobs to further your IT career?

☐ Are you prepared to learn new skills to meet the changing demand on the IT profession?

☐ Do you have a flexible approach to work? (Working in IT is not always a 9–5 job)

☐ Can you work to strict deadlines, without supervision in a high-pressured and challenging environment?

☐ Do you enjoy the challenge to continually improve systems using IT?

☐ Can you think logically and draw conclusions based on known events?

☐ Do you enjoy problem solving?

There can be few people around today who are not aware of the impact the information technology (IT) revolution has had on the way we live and work. Practically every important event in our working life now seems to involve the use of computer technology; withdrawing cash from the 'hole in the wall' in our bank, (known to the IT community as 'automatic teller machines'); booking a holiday; home entertainment – the list goes on and on.

This is great news for anyone thinking of a career in IT, regardless of whether they are seeking their first job or planning a change of career. Today's information systems industry is an exciting place to be working – the number of opportunities available within IT continues to grow and average salaries remain relatively high. Such is the demand for computing expertise, the IT industry is currently facing a skills shortage: there are not enough *skilled* people to satisfy the number of job vacancies. While there are many opportunities for experienced technicians and analysts, movement into these positions must be balanced by recruitment at the lower levels to maintain the appropriate levels of skill within the organisation.

There is no better time than now to consider a career in information technology and computing; awareness of the subject is at a high, with the Careers Service and IT employers coming together to help train people for jobs within the IT industry. With the help of IBM, there is now a National Vocational Qualification (NVQ) in information technology, designed to equip people with the IT skills this industry is currently so short of. Similarly, there are now many more opportunities to study computing and information technology in college and university. If you want a career in the computing and IT industry, then you should congratulate yourself on having already taken the first (and most important!) step – by reading this book.

How to use this book

This book will give you an up-to-date insight into the computing and IT industry, how it has developed into the lucrative and rewarding industry it is today and how it will develop in the future. The early chapters of the book will provide you with general information on the computing and information technology industry; the structure of the industry, the jobs available and how you should set out to achieve your goal – to gain a career in the computing and IT industry. Throughout this section, there will be a number of business profiles and case studies, examining in detail some of the major employers within the computer industry and, more importantly, explaining what people *really* do in IT, how they got there and what you need to do to if you want to work in a similar role.

The later chapters of the book will provide you with information on the qualifications available in IT and where you can study for them. Also included in this section are useful addresses of the many supporting organisations found within the IT industry and how they can help you.

This book can only give you a general guide to the many opportunities available for training and employment within the IT industry. If you follow the advice within it, you will be able to use your time well in planning a career in IT; however, you will still need to use other sources of information, the Careers Service in particular. Whatever you plan to do, plan for success.

2 What is computing and information technology?

It is said that if we could look at the aircraft flight deck of the future, we would see a computer, a man and a dog. The computer would fly the aircraft, the man would watch the computer and the dog would be there to bite the man should he dare to touch the controls of the aircraft! Whether you agree with this rather comical view of future aircraft flight or not, you can be sure of one thing – IT is here to stay and it will, without doubt, have a strong influence on the way we live and work for a very long time.

For many people, the computer industry is a bit of an unknown quantity; after all, over the last ten years it has been responsible for introducing an unbelievable amount of new phrases into our everyday language, such as the computer 'virus', the 'hacker' and the 'web–surfer'.

The field of computing science and its counterpart, information technology, are certainly vibrant, dynamic areas in which to work, but like most other occupations, life is not always the same as that portrayed in films and on TV. Working in computing and IT does not necessarily mean world-wide travel, fast cars and expense accounts – for some it means working 12-hour shifts, being on call for problems 24 hours a day and spending large amounts of time in stuffy, noisy computer rooms. That's not to say the computer industry isn't short of opportunity and reward – quite the opposite in fact, but from the law of averages, we won't *all* become the next Bill Gates, the Microsoft supremo, or Clive Sinclair, the entrepreneurial inventor whose ZX81 home microcomputer changed the future of computing overnight. If you want to plan for a successful career in computing and IT, then this book will show you how.

A brief history

Information Technology is the study of information and how we can use and process that information effectively, but it is nothing new. The first commercial computers were introduced in the 1940s following years of research both in the UK and USA. These colossal machines filled a room, consumed huge amounts of power and were very expensive to build. So great was the investment required, many experts believed only a few dozen computers would ever be needed.

The major breakthrough came with the development of the transistor; computers, although still relatively expensive to build, became smaller and more efficient. Further developments saw the introduction of the integrated circuit (IC) which allowed thousands of transistors and other electrical components to be 'printed' onto a piece of silicon – the silicon 'chip'. From that point onwards, the power of ICs has grown enormously (since the 1960s the number of components on a single chip has doubled every year), enabling computers to perform tasks which were once thought impossible.

Who uses information technology?

Over the last 40 years, the computer has moved from being a mathematical instrument used solely for scientific research, to a tool that can be used by anyone to perform all manner of tasks: playing games, controlling machinery and even diagnosing medical complaints! The use of computers within society is so widespread, it would be impossible to even consider a future without it. For every use of computers there is an opportunity for you to establish a career in that area; after all, *someone* has to write the computer game or financial spreadsheet program; and there is no reason why that person can't be you.

Home computing

Ever since the microcomputer revolution of the 1980s, home

purchases of personal computers (PCs) have risen significantly each year. In fact, private use of computing and information technology is rapidly out-pacing all the traditional areas of computing; already, over 50 per cent of the PCs sold are bought by people for home use. This trend is set to continue well into the future and the home market for computing is now as important in terms of sales and revenue as the commercial market.

Business computing

The most dramatic changes to have taken place in computing and IT have mainly been within the business sector. Over the last 40 years, many of the working practices traditionally found within business have been completely redesigned around computers, from the smallest of business operations to the largest of the multinational companies. Many organisations now use computers to perform traditionally manual administrative tasks such as producing sales and business documents, storing customer and order information and producing financial accounts. This is computing in its most simple form – replacing a manual procedure; the typewriter for the word-processor and the filing cabinet for the database.

Retailing

You only have to walk down to the local supermarket to discover how computer technology is now used within retailing. Our purchases are identified by a computerised 'bar-code' which allows the computerised supermarket till to provide us with an itemised bill, automatically calculating the total to allow for discounts, 'two for one' offers and so on. Similarly, many of these electronic tills now automatically print cheque details and accept credit cards for payment.

At the close of trading the computer system adopts a much more crucial role. At a set time each evening, the computer tills in the supermarket will transfer the information collected during the day (such as the number of items sold in a particular range) to the supermarket's central computer. This information will then be used to automatically order new levels of stock, so maintaining the correct stock level for any item sold in the store.

These specialised computer terminals, called Electronic Point-of-Sale (EPOS) systems have enabled the retail sector to reduce costs considerably and so become more efficient and profitable.

Finance

The financial sector is a huge user of computing technology; in fact, the worldwide financial markets are now completely dependent upon computer systems for their financial information.

During a typical day in the London Stock Exchange, millions of pounds transfer between investment companies within seconds, literally at the touch of a button. What happens behind the scenes is awesome in terms of computer power; thousands of people rely upon this computer system to provide accurate, up-to-date information every day. With the growth in the financial markets, eg banking, insurance and investment, the demand for better and faster computing systems can only increase dramatically.

The public sector

Government bodies, such as the Department of Social Security (DSS) and the Driver Vehicle Licensing Centre (DVLC), are renowned for generating and processing huge amounts of information. Information which was once held on paper is now stored on computer and accessed from computer terminals situated all over the country. Not only has the computer enabled workers in the public sector to improve their working practices, it has also enabled them to gain new skills in computing and information technology. Similarly, the use of computer systems in the public sector has also helped save the average tax-payer a great deal of money, by identifying the cleverly disguised and complex instances of fraud which were extremely difficult, if not impossible, to detect in the old, paper-based system.

The IT skills shortage

The UK computer industry currently employs more than 40,000 people. By the year 2000, this figure is expected to be over 500,000. Demand for computing and IT has never been higher, and is still growing. Job opportunities, especially for people new to the computing industry, have never been greater – already thousands of people join the computer industry every year, yet there is *still* a skills shortage within the profession.

The advance of IT has now generated a whole range of sophisticated software tools capable of building all manner of applications; unfortunately, there are not enough people within the computer industry with skills in these areas. While this is not good news for business, it is good news for anyone seeking a career in computing. Over the last five years or so, demand for certain skills has moved around as business tries to find new methods of solving the same problems. Table 2.1 shows the IT skills *currently* in demand, although it is fair to say that most of these will remain in demand well into the twenty-first century. As you can see from the table, all of the skills in the top ten are based on UNIX or Windows technology, with the exception of COBOL. Although this observation is a little bit surprising, it does, however, reflect the changes taking place within the industry. In Chapter 3 we will look more closely at how the structure of the IT industry has changed over the last 40 years and how you can plan for a career within it. One last point to mention about Table 2.1 (and one which will be mentioned in more detail in Chapter 3) is that none of the top 10 skills is related to any one specific computer manufacturer. In the early days of computing, many computer applications were linked to a particular manufacturer, eg IBM or ICL. Now the computer industry is moving away from these 'proprietary' systems to a more 'open' approach – hence the popular IT term, 'open systems'.

Table 2.1 *Skills most in demand (July 1996)*

Position (July 1996)	Skill	Category	Number of jobs
1	UNIX	Operating system + programming utilities	25,535
2	C++	programming language	21,634
3	C	programming language	19,983
4	Oracle	UNIX relational database application	17,431
5	Windows	PC operating system	13,842
6	COBOL	Commercial programming language	12,546
8	Windows NT	PC operating system	10,252
9	SQL	database query language	9,399
10	Novell	networking software	8,940
11	RPG400	programming language used on IBM AS/400 computers	8,898
12	DB2	IBM mainframe relational database application	6,487
13	LAN	Local area network activity	6,307
14	CICS	IBM mainframe commercial programming language	6,289
15	Microsoft Office	Windows-based application suite	4,807
16	Sybase	UNIX relational database application	4,554
17	TCP/IP	networking protocol	4,550
18	Lotus products	PC-based application software	3,690
19	Ingres	mainframe relational database application	3,477
20	Microsoft Access	Windows-based relational database application	3,420

(Source: SSP/*Computer Weekly* Quarterly Survey of Appointments Data and Trends)

One simple method used within the IT industry to gauge the demand for IT skills is to count the number of advertised jobs in the popular computer publications. One such publication, *Computer Weekly*, during the summer of 1996, published its largest ever issue since 1989; over the three month period, there were 33,500 jobs on offer. One report on the IT job market, compiled for another IT magazine, *Computing*, found that recruitment during the first few months of 1996 had already reached 40 per cent of the level for the whole of 1995! Based on the number of advertised job vacancies, the report concluded that the skill areas most in demand (ordered by the percentage of job adverts found) were:

◆ computer systems and network integration
◆ pre-sale and post-sale support
◆ database and systems administrators
◆ programmers
◆ network specialists.

This imbalance between supply and demand is forcing advertisers to increase the salaries on offer for the many IT positions. On average, the rate of salary increase found among IT professionals during 1996 was 5.4 percent – more than double the rate of inflation.Table 2.2 should give you a good idea of what sort of salaries to expect in the main job areas within IT. Don't forget, these figures are based on the 'transfer-value' of existing, experienced IT professionals, so the starting salaries for a first job will be considerable lower. Having said that, there are many London-based IT consultancy companies which are more than willing to pay £20,000 starting salaries to attract graduates in any discipline for their own training and development programme.

Table 2.2 *Average 1996 salaries for IT occupations*

Job Title	Average salary	Percentage change from 1995
IT Manager	£44,499	+8%
Systems Analyst	£25,586	+6%
Programmer	£19,746	+5%
Analyst Programmer	£23,138	+6%
PC Support Analyst	£20,776	+6%
Software Engineer	£25,197	+3%
Network Support Technician	£18,364	+7%
Computer Operator	£16,617	+11%

(Source: SSP/*Computer Weekly* Quarterly Survey of Appointments Data and Trends)

Is a professional qualification really necessary?

Anyone looking closely at the IT industry as a possible career option will soon discover there are many people employed within it who do not possess a degree, A-levels or even GCSE/O-levels. However, it is true to say that you will have a much better chance of getting a job if you do possess at least one or two A-levels. Even though there is currently a skills shortage within the IT industry, do not take this to mean you will find it any easier to gain the job you want. Competition is very fierce and over half of the people recruited into the industry already have degrees.

Many IT companies, both in the public and private sector, take the view that having a degree does not automatically make you an obvious choice for a job vacancy – in some cases it can even reduce your chances of a job. If a company wishes to employ a graduate, they will have to finance a relatively large initial invest-ment – in London that could be over £20,000 a year. For the company to then 'get their money's worth', they must keep that graduate on for as long as possible to benefit from their education and training. For some companies, this is a bit of a gamble, as the average turnover rate among IT graduates is still high – many leave within two years of getting their first IT job.

On the other hand, if the company recruits a school-leaver with GCSEs who has an active interest in computing, for about £10,000 a year, not only will they be saving a large amount of money, but they can also train that person to perform their role well. The employer benefits by keeping costs down while keeping lower-paid staff motivated, and the employee benefits by gaining marketable IT skills.

The IT industry is still split on this issue; some recruitment managers insist on a degree, others vigorously challenge the 'degree mentality', arguing that it is attitude and competence that matter, not a degree certificate. What is important though, is that the computer industry is short of people with *skills*, not qualifications. While gaining an academic qualification is one possible way of gaining suitable IT skills, it is not the only way; there are numerous opportunities available today for people to gain the skills they need to obtain employment within the IT industry, many of which are available all over the country. One thing, is clear, however: once you have gained a fair amount of experience, the emphasis placed on academic qualifications reduces.

3 Careers in computing and information technology

Today's IT industry is now relatively stable in terms of job security; since the minor recession the UK economy experienced in the early 1990s, computing and IT jobs have continued to remain in demand. No one can predict the future, but it does seem as though this increased demand for IT will remain with us well into the next century.

From the very beginnings of the commercial IT industry, in the 1960s, the development of IT was dominated by the manufacturing 'giants' of the computer world; business had little choice but to rely on them for all their computing requirements, such as application development and consultancy. Eventually their monopoly was successfully challenged, and a whole new generation of software suppliers and consultancy companies emerged as a result. Having fresh ideas on the future of IT, these new companies not only developed business applications for existing computer systems, they also helped introduce applications for the next generation of computers – and sparked off a way of thinking which was to revolutionise careers within the IT profession.

Choosing the right computer for the right job

When you start looking for employment within the IT industry, you will soon discover that the majority of job functions are specific to a particular type of computer – the computer 'platform' as it is called. For instance, if you were looking for a career providing support and advice to the users of a computer system, you would need to be aware of what 'platform' their application was running on; someone who has a lot of experience fixing PC problems will not be much use to someone experiencing difficulties on an IBM mainframe! The main computer platforms you need to be aware of are:

Super-computing

Often restricted to large-scale research and development work, 'super-computers' are mainly used when large numbers of mathematical calculations need to be performed in a relatively short space of time (a process known as 'number-crunching'). Super-computers are generally used for the following applications: processing weather information, processing large mathematical equations and performing complex simulations (war-games, flight simulators, etc).

Mainframe computing

Historically, commercial computing applications have been developed using large computer systems called 'mainframes'. Mainframes are typically used in organisations which require large amounts of processing power to achieve their required workload. Despite their size, mainframe computers are often connected together to increase the capacity of the computer system. Company payroll, stock control and order processing systems are just some of the applications found in mainframe computing.

Midrange computing

Large commercial departments often use a dedicated computer, sometimes called a 'mini-computer', capable of supporting about 100 users, solely for one or two critical applications, for instance, insurance premium management or financial planning. Midrange computing is becoming much more important in the IT industry, as high-performance machines are now being produced which directly compete with their more expensive mainframe neighbours. The mainstay of the midrange computer market is currently the IBM AS/400 range of computers.

Desktop computing

PCs are now becoming an everyday commodity owing to their enormous versatility and ease of use. This, coupled with their low price tag for a relatively high-performance computer, has meant their growth has been unstoppable. With software vendors, such as Microsoft, providing numerous applications for the PC, there seems little doubt that the desktop revolution is here to stay. Most PC systems in use today are based around the following operating systems: Microsoft Windows, Windows '95 and Microsoft NT. As you might expect, there are literally hundreds of off-the-shelf application packages available for these systems, ranging from word-processing software to musical composition and film-editing software.

The rise in client-server computing

During the 1980s, mainframe and mini-computer applications were accessed through simple or 'dumb' computer terminals. These terminals had no computing power of their own and were used for entering data into the central computer. With the introduction of the personal computer, the IT industry gradually combined the features of the PC with the processing power of the larger computers, such as the mainframe, and developed a framework which is now generally termed 'client-server computing' (see Figures 3.1 and 3.2). Although appearing initially complex, the whole idea behind client-server computing is extremely simple – which is one of the reasons why it has become such a popular option.

Large mainframe-type computers are very good at storing and processing huge amounts of information and, as they provide most of the information required by the user, they are referred to as the 'server system'. PCs, on the other hand, have very powerful graphical display capabilities and, in a network, are often called 'intelligent workstations'.

Unlike the mainframe 'dumb' terminals which are solely used for data entry, PC terminals can also be used for a variety of tasks, such as those involving the use of colour and complex graphics, hence the term 'intelligent'. This sophisticated display feature of the PC, combined with a 'mouse' instead of a keyboard, is known as the 'GUI' (Graphical User Interface – pronounced 'gooey').

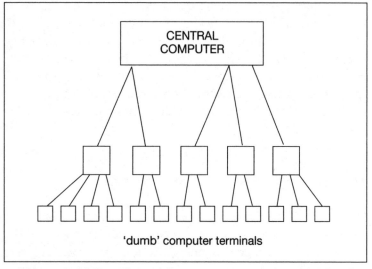

Figure 3.1 *The traditional way computer systems were developed in business*

When the PC is retrieving information from the server computer, for example, downloading information held on a central database and displaying it as a pie-chart through its GUI, it is acting as a 'client' on the network. Using a client-server system provides users with one major benefit – their work can be processed on the most appropriate platform available, which may not be the largest or most powerful computer on the network.

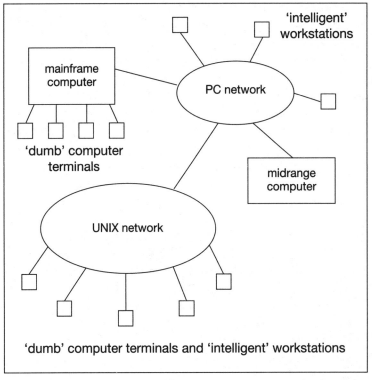

Figure 3.2 *The emerging way computer systems are developed in business – a typical client-server computer system*

The use of open systems

Application software is often written for one particular type of operating system running on a specific model of computer as it often uses features of that computer which are not found on other computers. Such a system is termed 'proprietary' as it is inextricably linked to the hardware manufacturer. There are, of course, many exceptions to this rule; many PC-based applications will run on any model of PC as long as it is running the Microsoft operating system; applications written for IBM mainframe computers will run on any IBM-compatible mainframe made by different hardware manufacturers as long as it is running an IBM mainframe operating system.

Luckily for business, the IT industry has spent the last ten years trying to move away from proprietary systems by developing an 'open systems' strategy to systems development. These computer systems, originally based on the UNIX operating system, have been developed by a consortium of leading computer hardware and software suppliers, their aim being quite simple – to agree a set of standards to which all the different computer suppliers can adhere when developing new systems. The benefits of this approach are enormous; computer systems and application software can be used almost interchangeably without any problems.

In theory, the open systems approach is a fine idea which, to its credit, has been welcomed with open arms by the IT industry. In practice, it is not short of problems. For instance, one report investigating the standardisation of open systems suggested there were already 26 different types of UNIX operating system available! Don't be misled though: open systems herald a new era in computing and any future developments in this field will probably use some of the following components:

◆ UNIX operating system
◆ 'C' programming language
◆ 'C++' programming language
◆ Java programming language
◆ 'Open' database products

PROFILE: A high street travel agency

The following example is designed to help you decide which particular area of IT might suit you best by briefly outlining the main components of a typical computer system (Table 3.1). There is no particular reason for picking a travel agent computer system for this example; all computer systems are basically the same.

Any computer system must have at least one processor which performs the real 'work', a number of storage devices to allow programs and data to be stored and protected when the computer is turned off, and a way of entering and retrieving data from the computer. Fundamentally, all that change are the programs which are run on the computer, as it is these which determine the application the computer system is used for. This is an important point to remember, as it is certainly one of the main benefits of working in the computer industry – flexibility.

Table 3.1 *Components of the travel agent computer system*

Computer hardware:	IT careers:
airline company mainframe computer	hardware designer
flight company mainframe computer	digital circuit engineer
travel agent PCs	hardware assembly technician
Computer software:	**IT careers:**
airline company flight reservation system	computer programmer
holiday company booking system	systems analyst
travel agent holiday booking/information system	computer tester
Computer network:	**IT careers:**
communications links between mainframe and PC	network engineer
travel agent PC LAN	network systems programmer
	network installer

Most application programs are written in the same way, regardless of the particular computer programming 'language' used (BASIC, C, COBOL, for instance). Most competent programmers can therefore program in a number of different languages just by reading the programming manual for that particular language. If you can do this, you will never be short of work in the IT industry.

Why is a computer system needed in the travel agency?

◆ To check the availability of holidays and flights.
◆ To reserve rooms in hotels throughout the world.

◆ To reserve seats on scheduled and chartered flights.
◆ To search for the most appropriate holidays for the customer.
◆ To find the best deal for the customer.
◆ To send details of all bookings made to the appropriate holiday companies.
◆ To process the end-of-day accounts.

The structure of the IT industry

Table 3.2 outlines the main areas of employment within the IT industry. As you can see, each area performs a number of business-related tasks which are often duplicated in other areas. This is not uncommon within the vast number of occupational areas in the IT industry, and it is yet another example of the flexibility and ease of movement which makes an IT career seem attractive when compared against other professions. Throughout this section, each of these will be discussed in turn so you can understand more fully the structure of the IT industry and, ultimately, how you can find employment within it.

Hardware manufacturers

Despite the boom in software both for the home and business over the last few years, the hardware market is still a substantial area within the IT industry. In 1993, the European computer market was estimated at £130 billion and growing. One-third of this total was spent with the hardware manufacturers.

During the early days of computing, the majority of the computer market was dominated by the larger IT companies, such as IBM and ICL, who were, in fact, hardware suppliers. Today's market has changed rapidly, and the IT industry has adopted a more 'open' approach. Customers are no longer expected to buy their computer systems from only one manufacturer – they can go to any number of similar vendors.

Table 3.2 *The structure of the IT industry*

Hardware manufacturers	Software and services suppliers	Value added resellers	Facilities management
computer design	programming	hardware sales	programming
component manufacture	marketing	software sales	technical support
electronics	systems analysis	design consultancy	helpdesk operations
assembly	systems design	programming	computer operations
testing	sales	networking design	hardware maintenance
marketing	business services		
sales			

Communications companies	IT users	Allied professions	Education
manufacture	programming	publishing	teaching
installation	systems analysis	medicine	lecturing
configuration	systems design	manufacturing	research
testing	user support	military	computer support
network design	user training	finance	business consultancy
network support		engineering	

Similarly, the hardware manufacturers now have the choice of adopting 'open' standards for chip design, interfaces and networking capability, allowing them to provide integrated solutions with other computer manufacturers.

Who produces what?

Computers, regardless of shape, size or cost, rely upon silicon chips for their operation. As the demand for yet more powerful computers increases, so too will the need for specialists capable of designing and manufacturing these complex integrated circuits. Almost 90 per cent of the high-performance chips found within large midrange and mainframe computers are produced by Japanese-owned companies, such as Fujitsu and Mitsubishi, while the circuits found within most PCs are produced largely by American manufacturers such as Intel and Motorola.

It is worth remembering that careers in computer system manufacture involve a great deal more than just designing and testing integrated circuits for use within the computer. All computer systems are worthless unless there is some means of entering data and extracting information. Every computer system, therefore, has a number of associated devices attached to it, called peripherals, which include equipment such as printers, computer screens and storage devices. There may also be networking and telecommunication equipment attached to the computer to allow information to be routed to another computer anywhere in the world. Computer peripherals are manufactured throughout the world, including the UK and the rest of Europe.

Career prospects

Computer hardware manufacturers can offer a number of highly skilled career structures which cover every aspect of the electronics manufacturing process from design to distribution. While these companies seek to employ highly-skilled professionals, there are always opportunities at all levels for people with fewer qualifications. It is more often the case that a basic understanding of electronics and physics is all that is required for many of the 'entry-level' opportunities within this area, as most if not all of the manufacturers have their own specific training and education programmes to develop expertise within the company. For example, two of the major hardware suppliers in the industry, IBM and ICL, both support the NVQ system of on-the-job training and accreditation.

Qualifications

If you want to enter the highly skilled areas of computer manufacture such as microprocessor and digital electronic technology at a professional level, you will normally require, at a minimum, education to A-level standard in subjects such as electronics, maths and computing. Even then, you will always face competition from those who have gained a degree in relevant subjects, such as computer science, digital electronics and manufacturing and computing. Many of the larger computer manufacturers have extremely good graduate training programmes and so can take graduates on in *any* discipline – yet more competition for those without a degree, unfortunately.

If you want to enter this field at an 'entry' level, having a support and administration role as opposed to a design and construction role, you will often need no more than a GCSE-level of education. What is important at this level is having an active interest in computer design and manufacture and the ability to learn new skills. For example, the following list of skills would be considered very worthwhile for a junior position in computer design and manufacture:

◆ an interest in electronics, especially digital electronics
◆ an interest in building, customising and fixing computers
◆ an understanding of 'low-level' computer programming
◆ the ability to reason rationally and logically
◆ the ability to communicate technical issues to non-technical colleagues.

PROFILE: IBM UK

IBM UK is a subsidiary of the IBM Corporation, which is one of the world's largest suppliers of information technology hardware, software, solutions and services. IBM is truly a world-wide IT company, providing solutions to customers in over 130 countries. Within the UK, IBM has sites at more than 25 locations, including Basingstoke, Bedfont Lakes, Greenock, Hursley, London, Portsmouth, Manchester and Warwick.

Main activities
◆ Development and maintenance of computer software and hardware.
◆ Consultancy.
◆ Marketing.
◆ Manufacturing.

IBM Manufacturing
All the manufacturing by IBM in the UK is carried out at their Greenock site in Scotland. IBM employs more than 3,000 people at this site in a wide variety of manufacturing and technical roles ranging from high-volume assembly to IT management.

IBM Greenock is responsible for the development, manufacture and support of PCs for the European, Middle Eastern and African markets, and is the only site within IBM world-wide where design, manufacture and support are completely integrated. Already they employ over 250 overseas staff who manage the customer's order from manufacture to delivery. This is carried out for 76 countries in 17 different languages. One of the most popular IBM products, the award-winning IBM ThinkPad, is manufactured entirely at Geenock.

Qualifications required
IBM accepts graduates from many disciplines, ranging from scientific and computing areas to the arts. As you would expect from a company with such a wide range of career options, IBM can offer employment at all levels; and for the more technical positions, it welcomes graduates with Masters degrees. Having

operations throughout the world, it is particularly keen to recruit IT professionals with language skills as well as technical skills. IBM regularly advertises at recruitment fairs and exhibitions throughout the year.

Contact
Recruitment Services, IBM UK, PO Box 41, North Harbour, Portsmouth, Hants PO6 3AU

PROFILE: Intel Ireland Ltd

Intel Ireland is a subsidiary of the massive Intel Corporation, one of the market leaders in microprocessor design and manufacture. They are easily one of the major IT companies to invest in Ireland, with over $1 billion invested in their Ireland operation by the end of 1995.

Intel's manufacturing complex in County Kildare is the company's sole manufacturing centre for Europe, with three factories on-site and a fourth under construction. The company directly employs over 2,800 people, with another 800 people being employed on-site by other service companies.

Main activities
- ◆ Manufacture of semi-conductor products (eg Pentium processor).
- ◆ Manufacture of PC motherboards.
- ◆ Manufacture of PCs and servers for leading computer vendors.
- ◆ PC maintenance and repair.

Qualifications required
Over one third of Intel employees are graduates. However, due to the wide-ranging skills used within the company, graduates are recruited from many disciplines, such as electronic engineering, mechanical engineering, computer science and information technology. As you would expect from a company whose operations are so widespread, Intel can offer employment at all levels within

the company; as a minimum, they recruit entry-level employees with five passes on their Leaving Certificate (the Irish equivalent of A-levels).

Intel readily accept 'on-spec' CVs for current and future positions – these are scanned electronically and stored on their recruitment database. Should a vacancy exist (Intel are currently recruiting heavily) the database is searched and a short-list drawn up.

Contact
Personnel Department, Intel Ireland Ltd, Collinstown Industrial Park, Leixlip, County Kildare, Ireland; 01606 7000

Software and services suppliers

Of all the areas within the IT industry, the software and services sector is the one which employs the most people and one which can offer the most opportunities for first-time recruits into the profession. Its size and importance in terms of employment potential means the software and services sector is an area you should consider very carefully before embarking on any specific career path.

In 1994, the European software and computing services market was the second largest market in the world, and growing at a rate of nearly 6 per cent a year. It is estimated that over 16,000 software and services companies with over 300,000 employees exist within Western Europe. The vast majority of these have less than 20 employees and several of those companies have no more than five employees. Of the larger software and services companies, most of these are located in the UK.

It is hardly surprising, therefore, to find that the UK is now the fastest growing market in Europe for the software and services industry according to the latest financial reports. This is good news for anyone wanting a career in programming, whether it be application software, software for military purposes or operating-system level programming.

While the main computing function in this area is centred upon programming, this area of IT also provides business with a number of computer-related services, which can involve supporting and developing any part of a company's IT operations, including hardware, software, telecommunications and management consultancy. The different kinds of software and services activities found within IT can usually be split into the following categories:

Application software development

This category is focused primarily on developing and supporting the computer programs which provide solutions to specific business problems. These companies are not interested in computer hardware or operating systems – they are interested in increasing their profitability by selling computer programs and computer services, such as business consultancy.

It has been said, 'Without software, the most powerful computer in the world is just a hunk of metal'; it might sound a bit tongue-in-cheek, but there is more than a grain of truth in it. Using the right software, people employed within the business (the computer 'users') can increase productivity while keeping costs down – good news for the company balance sheet. Despite these exciting new software developments, very few users of computers (especially management!) are bothered how the computer system actually works, as long as it does the job it is intended for. Should the computer software fail for any reason, managers will suddenly take a very active interest in the computer system and the computer 'trouble-shooting' team (often called 'technical support' or 'application support') will be asked to come and fix the computer system or the software running on it.

Typical examples of application software systems would include:

◆ airline reservation systems
◆ stock-control systems
◆ financial accounts packages
◆ word-processing, spreadsheet and database packages
◆ newspaper and magazine editing software.

Systems software development

There are two main programming areas within this category: operating system development and systems software development. Within any computer, there must be programs which control the various devices attached to it, such as computer screens, printers and storage devices. Similarly, every computer must have routines to perform tasks such as scanning the keyboard for input and scheduling work for the central processing unit (CPU). Collectively, these programs are known as the computer's 'operating system'. Development and support work on the computer operating system is a complex and highly technical task and is therefore usually only performed by a computer system manufacturer.

While computer software is written for the users of the computer system, software is also used by technical experts who support, maintain and develop the computer system itself. In a technical support environment, many specialist programs are used to perform a wide variety of diagnostic functions, such as identifying potential performance and capacity problems on the computer system. If the technical support staff had to perform these complex tasks themselves, it would take a considerable amount of time, which is often the one resource you never have enough of in a trouble-shooting role. Specialist computer software which is used by technicians as opposed to users is often called 'systems software'. Typical system software used on all the major computer platforms provides technical staff with the following:

◆ computer performance and tuning software
◆ database maintenance software
◆ software to take backups of programs
◆ security or 'access-control' software used to prevent unauthorised access to computer systems
◆ diagnostic software used to detect network-related errors.

Bureau services

This category provides business with specific computing services, such as processing monthly payroll information, which is originally entered onto a magnetic computer tape by the organisation's payroll staff and then sent to the computer bureau. The bureau would then process the information and produce the organisation's accounts and payroll information for that month. Bureau companies provide a useful service to organisations which do not want to invest huge sums of money in computer systems for which they only have a limited use.

Consultancy and service providers

As the number of applications, technologies and strategies delivered by the IT industry increases, so too does the number of options available to business – the customer. For instance, what computer platforms should an organisation develop in order to expand its IT capability? Mainframe? UNIX? PC? Equally what database application should it use for its customer accounts department? IBM's DB2? Oracle? Microsoft Access? There are, of course, hundreds of other questions which organisations in this position would want to ask – how to build the most appropriate computer network for instance. None of these questions can be answered easily without understanding the organisation's specific business requirements, both in the short-term and in the long-term (computer systems can become obsolete very quickly, so some thought must be taken when deciding on any strategy).

For example, consider the directors of a brewery who want to know how to expand their current computer system to cope with the addition of 200 more pubs. As company directors, they probably know quite a lot about the brewing and catering business, but not so much about information technology. This is where the IT consultancy companies and services flourish – they do know quite a lot about the IT industry, its products, strategies and technologies. These companies work closely with the customer (in this example, the brewery) to identify all their requirements and the best ways of achieving them. The main functions found within the IT consultancies and service providers will therefore be focused around designing, developing and implementing these requirements using whatever computer hardware and software they feel is necessary.

Software development in action

There is never a shortage of business problems throughout the world which cannot be solved by computer software, which is why a career within software development can be such an interesting one. When writing business software, it is crucial that you first understand the needs and requirements of the business and are able to identify the technical solution necessary to solve their problems. This is a lengthy process which starts with a business requirement and ends with a delivered computer solution – it is called the 'software development life cycle' and is shown in Table 3.3.

Career prospects

There are very good career prospects for people wanting to work for the software companies; programmers continue to remain in demand at all levels from junior programmers working for local government to software development consultants working for large multinational companies. If you are technically-oriented, then a career working for the systems and application software companies seems an obvious choice. These companies are generally large and sited centrally, so you may have to consider location when deciding – are you willing to move to find the job you want? Consultancy and service companies on the other hand tend to be much smaller in size and more geographically dispersed. In these companies, while being technical in nature, focus is also placed on teamwork and 'people skills', as communication at all levels will be necessary.

Qualifications

The sheer size of the software and services industry means that there are job opportunities at all levels within it. If you want to walk straight into a consultancy role with one of the major computer service providers (eg Cap Gemini, EDS, Price-Waterhouse) you will, without doubt, need a good degree. If the employer also has a graduate training programme, you will not necessarily need a degree in a computing subject – they will train you for whatever role you are best suited to.

Table 3.3 *The stages of the systems development life cycle, and the IT careers they relate to*

Stage	Tasks	IT job title
Feasibility study	understanding user requirements (what is the problem?) document current system, talk to users write reports	business systems analyst
Requirements analysis	propose new solution define requirements plan project timescales	business systems analyst
Requirements Definition	high-level design of system implementation planning	business systems designer
System design	program design application design database design	business systems designer
Construction	write programs use application tools test	programmer/ systems developer system tester
Implementation	train users write technical documentation	computer trainer technical author
Support	fix computer problems control the computer help users with problems	technical support computer operator computer help desk

PROFILE: Oracle Corporation

The Oracle Corporation is the world's largest supplier of database software and information management software, with annual revenues of over $4.2 billion. Oracle software, while often associated with UNIX systems, runs on almost every computer, from the smallest laptop to the massively powerful super-computers. Oracle software is designed to support all stages of software development, by providing tools that will help the systems analyst design and model business systems and the programmer design and develop the database and data-entry screens.

Scope of operation: 93 countries worldwide
Number of staff: 25,000+
Revenue (1996): over $4.2 billion
Profit (1996): over $600 million

Key products:
Relational database software (Oracle 7).
Systems modelling software (Designer/2000), used for modelling a business and generating database applications
Application development software (Developer/2000)
Internet development software (WebServer), supporting the development of Web applications using languages such as Java and C++

Key business areas:
Software development
Education and training
Customer support
Consultancy

Career Opportunities
Oracle UK recruit graduates from many disciplines in addition to computer science, all having proven academic success in a relevant area. Normally only 10 per cent of applicants are invited for an interview, during which candidates will be expected to sit psychometric tests. There is no formal recruitment policy, and students with A-levels can apply for positions, as can school-leavers, normally as part of a youth training scheme.

Contact

Human Resources Department, Oracle UK Corporation Limited, Oracle Parkway, Thames Valley Park, Reading, Berkshire, RG6 1RA; Tel: 0118 924 0000

PROFILE: Cap Gemini

Cap Gemini is the number one provider of consulting and IT services in Europe and the number three provider world-wide. It was founded over 20 years ago by the merger of three computer services and consulting companies: CAP, Gemini Computer Services and Sogeti.

Scope of operation: world-wide. Operations in 15 European countries, USA and the Far East
Number of staff: 30,000+
Revenue (1995): over US $4.2 billion

Key business activities:
Computer systems and management consultancy
Computer systems integration
Development and implementation

Key customers:
Major corporations
Specialist organisations
Government agencies

Business areas:
Management consulting
Information technology Services

The Cap Gemini Group provides a broad range of services which can be organised into five main areas:

◆ consulting
◆ project services
◆ software products

◆ information systems management
◆ education and training

Career opportunities
To work at a professional level within Cap Gemini you will need a degree; this can be in any subject. Candidates will be expected to sit an aptitude test as part of the recruitment process.

Entry into this level is possible without a degree if candidates possess at least 18 months'–two years' experience in a particular IT field. As with many large companies, there are 'entry-level' opportunities for people who do not possess a degree. These are mainly based around providing a 'help-desk' support role for the desktop environment within the company (PCs, Windows, etc). Cap Gemini does not take people on straight from school.

Contact
Recruitment Services, CAP Gemini UK PLC, Cap Gemini House, 95 Wandsworth Road, London, SW8 2HG; 0171 735 0800

Recruitment Services, Cap Gemini Ireland, 20–22 Lower Hatch Street, Dublin 2; 01666 13266

Value added resellers

Alongside the huge growth in software development is the equally phenomenal growth in the number of companies known as 'solutions providers' or value added resellers (VARs). These companies work closely with the customer, often providing a comprehensive systems development service, from system design to implementation. VARs provide a very welcome service to the business as they act as the 'middle-man' between the business and the computer vendor. The VAR will recommend software and hardware to meet the customer's requirements, supply and install products and provide an after-sales service to help fix any problems that might develop. Historically, this service was only provided by the computer hardware and software suppliers which, although technically expert, were not always focused on the customer and their specific requirements. All this has now changed for the better within the IT profession, and emphasis is now heavily focused on providing the customer with value-for-money computer systems, rather than just providing them with the latest off-the-shelf products.

Key services provided by VARs:

◆ consultancy
◆ networking (recommending networking hardware and software)
◆ application development (design and programming)
◆ product installation and configuration (computer hardware, software and networking products)
◆ training (customer training, technical training)
◆ support (fixing problems, providing a helpdesk function for customers who contact them with problems in either using or developing the computer system).

PROFILE: Tertio Limited

Scope of operation: UK only
Number of staff: 100+

Principal areas of operation:
   Consultancy
   Network management
   Systems management

Key business partnerships:
   Hewlett Packard (computer manufacturer and software supplier)
   Remedy (US-based software supplier)
   Microsoft (software supplier)
   Bay Networks (networking software supplier)

Tertio is a relatively small, but rapidly expanding, computer solutions provider with offices in London (head office), Manchester and Bath. Working closely with leading end computer companies, it develops a wide range of products used by some of the largest companies in the business world. Systems development work is focused on customer-oriented projects, involving work in all areas of the systems development life cycle. This is a customer-focused role, involving a high degree of contact with the customer. Understanding customer requirements and explaining technical solutions in an appropriate way is critical in this type of role.

Qualifications expected
Over 90 per cent of Tertio employees have degrees. It has a strong preference for computer science graduates, but also recognises that experience in key skill areas is acceptable for some positions within the company.

Required skills
◆ Strong technical ability (programming, networking, systems design).
◆ Client-presentable.
◆ Good business awareness (what are the current technologies? What are the future developments in IT?)
◆ Good problem-solving skills – a logical, rational thinker.
◆ Articulate – able to communicate at a technical level and at a customer level.
◆ Good at listening and understanding.

Placement opportunities
Students at university can apply for a period of work experience at Tertio.

Contact
Tertio Limited, 1 Angel Square, Torrens Street, London, EC1V 1NY; 0171 843 4000

Facilities management

Many of the leading IT service suppliers have a specialist division which will manage any computer-related operation; from supporting an order-processing system written in COBOL to the running of an entire computing department. This important service is known as *facilities management* and as many companies are now reviewing their 'non-core' IT operations, this area is likely to increase dramatically in the future.

Communications companies

Computer communications deals with the exchange of electronic information between computers and other electronic devices. Over the last five years this field has seen phenomenal growth as more and more companies seek to expand their computer operations both nationally and internationally. When computer users connect their computers in this way, it is termed a 'network' and it allows users to share information and data between machines, using some form of physical link such as a fibre-optic cable. Networks can range from the small departmental local-area networks (LANs) to networking spanning continents: wide-area networks (WANs).

One of the networking areas constantly in the news today is the Internet, which is simply the interconnection of many individual networks into one large global system. Huge amounts of information can now be retrieved from practically anywhere in the world with ease, which as well as providing many people with a few hours of enjoyment, is also providing the business world with new opportunities in world-wide sales and marketing. A particularly good example of the rapid growth in international network communications is the World Wide Web, probably the most dominant of all the 'Internet' applications around today.

Communications, or 'networking' as it is sometimes called, covers a huge span of products and technologies, including telecommunication products, computer hardware and computer software. Likewise, it spans an equally large range of technical areas, including digital electronics, audio and video, computing and network design (cabling and configuration). The companies involved in computer communications are typically either equipment manufacturers or suppliers or networking consultants, providing advice and assistance during and after the installation and configuration of the computer network.

PROFILE: Case Technology

Case Technology (formerly part of Cray Communications) is one of the leading manufacturers of advanced networking products in Europe. Having over 20 years' experience of computer networking, the company now has about 30 per cent of the UK market.

Scope of operation: six sales offices and partners in over 65 countries

Number of staff: 500, with 40 engineers working in research and development in the UK

Key business areas:
Design of computer WAN networking equipment
Manufacture of networking products
Sales of communication equipment for voice, data and video networks

---

Placement opportunities
Case has a placement scheme allowing local school children short-term work experience, either in a technical or administrative role.

University research opportunities
Case sponsors research fellowships at Durham University (networking modelling) and Manchester University (voice systems).

Qualifications required
Dependent upon entry level. There is no set minimum qualification – students with a wide variety of qualifications, including GCSEs and A-levels, as well as graduates are welcome to apply for positions within the company. For employment within IT areas, potential employees will be asked to sit numeric and verbal reasoning tests to prove competence in certain areas.

Contact
Marketing Department, Case Technology, Caxton Way, Watford Business Park, Watford, Hertfordshire, WD1 8XH

IT users

Computing and information technology is now used in practically every business organisation that contains an office. The use of IT in business is enormously varied – the local corner shop might possess a single computer terminal to process national lottery tickets whereas huge multinational companies might invest millions in the latest IT and global communication systems. Both types of organisations, however, are using IT for the same reason: to improve their business, either by increasing revenue or by improving important business functions, such as stock-control and order-processing. IT users form an important part of the IT community as they are the ones who will decide whether or not to use the latest technology available. If they prefer to stay with the current 'tried and tested' technologies, many hardware and software suppliers risk losing a lot of money in their investment.

PROFILE: The Post Office

The Post Office is one of the biggest (and earliest) users of information technology in the UK and makes use of a very wide range of computing technologies and methods. It has a central IT unit (with about 1,000 people based in Farnborough, Hants, and Chesterfield, Derbyshire) which provides support and services across the Post Office businesses, and there are many more people working on computerised systems within those businesses.

The central unit provides IT career opportunities at three levels.

A-level school-leavers are recruited to posts in the computer operations departments and may be carrying out jobs such as running batch programmes on mainframe computers, or taking and dealing with calls on the Post Office IT help desks; once they have more knowledge of computing, many of them move into more specialist jobs.

Degree students (not necessarily on computing or IT courses) can apply for a limited number of places with the Post Office during or shortly after their last year. Those selected are put through a carefully designed programme of training courses and six-month placements in different departments, with the intention of preparing them to become the senior specialists and managers of the future.

The other group of IT people joining the Post Office are those who have already gained some knowledge and experience elsewhere. With the size and range of IT activities in the Post Office, there is a steady demand for new people and promotion can be very fast for the right people. Salary arrangements and other benefits for IT people have to be more flexible than is usual in large organisations to ensure that the Post Office can compete successfully in the very busy and fast-moving IT job market.

Contact
The Post Office, IT Services, Concept 2000, 250 Farnborough Road, Farnborough, Hants GU14 7LU; 01252 528000

Allied professions – printing and publishing

Over the last 15 years there have been massive changes throughout this profession, affecting the publishing and distribution of newspapers, magazines and books, the majority of it resulting from the introduction of computing and information technology. For instance, front-page headlines are no longer manually typeset, but edited using desktop publishing (DTP) software on a PC.

It is worth remembering that today's publishing industry is not solely based on the use of paper – the use of magnetic media such as CD-ROM and the Internet is now becoming equally important. With the rising use of video and sound to enhance what was previously a largely text-based industry, this new field of 'multimedia' applications will mean there will be a need for highly-skilled IT specialists to help develop these new applications for home and business use. Fundamentally, these new IT roles are based around software development, much of which is already beginning to take place in the UK, as well as in the USA, where companies such as Microsoft are leading the way.

Career prospects

Apart from the technical support roles which can be found in any organisation using computers, there are now many new opportunities to fulfil a career in the printing and publishing profession using computer technology. There are many different aspects of printing and publishing which now require computer skills as well as traditional skills, such as typesetting, colour overlaying and electronic imaging. These are demanding jobs in a dynamic environment which will appeal to anyone who likes not only 'computing with words', but also audio and video too. It is without doubt a career which will encompass many professions and skills.

PROFILE: EMAP Construct

EMAP Construct is part of EMAP plc, a leading UK publisher of professional and business magazines, with over 65 titles and directories on its publishing list, many of which are market leaders in their particular category.

EMAP plc

Scope of operation: international, with offices in the UK, France, Germany and Switzerland
Number of staff: 5000+ (20 per cent of whom work in mainland Europe)
Revenue (1997): £741.6m
Profit (1997): £121.1m

Key business areas:
    Technical support for computer users
    Computer programming
    Internet development
    All aspects of publishing (page formatting, document composition, etc)

Career opportunities

EMAP Construct supports work experience schemes, mainly catering for the 18–25 age group during further and higher education. Placement periods last from two weeks to three months. Most of the experience offered is project-related and will involve work with database software. The objective of the placements is to offer valuable work experience to anyone who is interested in a career in IT support or in database management.

Qualifications expected

Educated to Advanced GNVQ/A-level standard.

Placement skills desired

◆ Ability to work with people.
◆ Knowledge of Microsoft Office.
◆ Knowledge of PC-based database packages (Filemaker Pro, Paradox).
◆ Knowledge of Netware 3.11 (PC-LAN networking software).
◆ Good organisational skills.

Contact

EMAP Construct, 151 Rosebery Avenue, London, EC1R 4QX; 0171 505 6760

Allied professions – manufacturing and engineering

Despite accusations of favouring the more traditional methods of work, there is a long history of computers and IT being used in the manufacturing and engineering profession, many of them extremely complex and state-of-the-art. The challenges facing the industry to exploit computer technology as we move into the next millennium mean the manufacturing and engineering profession will continue to offer many new and exciting opportunities for those seeking a career within IT.

One such technology is computer-aided engineering (CAE)

which combines the design and manufacturing process into a system which is controlled directly by sophisticated computer systems. Separately, the process which supports the industrial design operation, such as model-building, technical drawing and simulation is called computer-aided design (CAD). CAD systems generally feature a computer running sophisticated drawing and design software which in turn is connected to one or more high-resolution display screens. As you might expect, the process which supports the manufacturing operation is called computer-aided manufacturing (CAM). CAM systems typically involve the use of high-performance, computer-controlled industrial robots, such as those depicted in many car manufacturers' adverts on TV.

Career prospects

Manufacturing presents many diverse opportunities for professionals in both the manufacturing and IT professions, encompassing everything from plant operation to leading-edge research and development. The larger companies tend to have a computing department which works closely with the manufacturing operation, providing IT solutions to the business. Smaller companies may have just a few IT experts working within a manufacturing team, providing more specialised assistance, such as programming industrial robots used in the manufacturing process.

An alternative career path for those interested in using their IT skills in the manufacturing industry can be followed by working for a software supplier which specialises in designing and writing computer software for the manufacturing industry. For example, CAD systems use software tools which allow the operator to electronically 'draw and design' the product on the computer screen. These programs are extremely complex, requiring a high level of skill in writing complex, low-level programs. Being vastly different from writing commercial software, such as order-processing systems, this programming field is often termed 'software engineering'.

Getting started

At a professional level it is not uncommon to find manufacturing staff with qualifications in both computing and manufacturing engineering. The need for multi-skilled professionals in this area is now becoming greater and greater as the manufacturing industries seek to gain market advantage by exploiting IT in a similar way to commercial sector.

Due to the constant need for research into new manufacturing methods and technologies (such as materials science for instance), many manufacturing companies now have strong research links with universities and actively sponsor university research programmes.

For those people who see a career in IT and manufacturing as a means of entering senior management, there are a number of higher degrees available (MSc, MEng) which can be undertaken after gaining a degree in either an IT-related subject or a manufacturing-related subject. These advanced courses are often run at specialist institutes where students are exposed to leading-edge research and development while understanding the management implications of these types of projects.

Typical skills required

◆ Usually a degree in engineering/computing (the British Computer Society is affiliated to the Institute of Chartered Engineers and can award its members professional engineering qualifications).

◆ Programming languages such as 'C', which can be used for controlling machinery and processes while they are running ('real-time' applications).

◆ Low-level high-speed programming languages such as Assembler.

Education

See Chapter 4 for details on teaching computing and IT skills.

4 Computing in education

With the focus often placed on business and commerce, it is easy to forget the crucial role IT plays within the academic world and the career opportunities that exist within it. IT skills are as much in demand within the educational system as they are in the commercial sector.

It is worth remembering that the computer scientists of the future will need to be educated *today* in order for them to fulfil their potential, and thanks to various strategic initiatives taken by the Department for Education and Employment, computing and IT now have a major part to play in education. Information technology is taught as part of the National Curriculum from primary school upwards and is in fact the only fundamentally *new* subject in the National Curriculum. In further and higher education, more and more computing-related subjects are being introduced all the time to meet the demands of business and commerce as well as for future research activity.

Opportunities to teach computing and information technology mainly exist from secondary school upwards; the main institutions which fall into this category are shown in Table 4.1. Information technology *is* taught in primary education, but to teach at this level, you will first need to learn specialised teaching methods and be able to teach in a wide range of other subjects as well as information technology.

Table 4.1 *The number of academic institutions teaching computing and IT (1994/5)*

Academic Institution	Number
Secondary schools	4478
City Technology Colleges (CTCs)	15
Further education (FE) colleges	587
Sixth-form colleges	114
Universities	110

Working in secondary education

If you want to teach information technology in a state-maintained secondary school you must first become a qualified teacher. This can be achieved in a number of different ways, but they will all provide you with, at minimum, qualified teacher status (QTS).

In most cases, QTS is achieved by following an approved course of initial teacher training (ITT). Around 30,000 places are available each year for ITT courses and, of those, about 14,000 are for secondary education training. Before you start your ITT course, you must have already gained the equivalent of GCSE grade C (or above) in both English language and mathematics. The two main routes to obtain QTS are by completing a degree course or a postgraduate course. These courses are run in schools, colleges and universities throughout the UK

Degree courses for teacher training

Any one of the following degrees will enable you to enter the teaching profession while also providing you with a professional qualification. They are all usually four years in length, combining a standard degree with a year of teacher training:

◆ BEd (Bachelor of Education – shortened two-year course also available)

◆ BA (Bachelor of Arts) with QTS
◆ BSc (Bachelor of Science) with QTS.

The basic minimum requirements for teacher training degrees are:

◆ five different subjects (grade C or above) at GCSE level or equivalent, including English language and mathematics
◆ two of which must be at A-level or equivalent, such as BTEC National award or GNVQ (General National Vocational Qualification) in computing or IT.

Postgraduate courses for teacher training

For secondary school teaching, the main route is by gaining a PGCE (Postgraduate Certificate in Education) qualification after you have obtained a degree through the normal routes (your degree, however, must contain a strong element of computing or IT). The standard PGCE is a one-year full-time course which you can enrol on either immediately after gaining your degree or return to after gaining a number of years' work experience. A PGCE for secondary education normally takes one academic year (36 weeks) to complete, including a minimum of 24 weeks' teacher training in a secondary school. There are some PGCE courses which are specific for those wanting to teach information technology at secondary school level, others contain a mixture of IT and other sciences to help reinforce the requirements laid down in the National Curriculum.

Open University PGCE

The Open University (OU) now runs distance-learning PGCE courses for secondary courses in IT subjects. These usually take 18 months to complete, combining periods of teaching practice and on-site school projects, making them comparable with a standard PGCE.

Postgraduate training routes

You can study for a PGCE at the following academic institutions:

◆ University or college of higher education
◆ School or City Technology College (school-centred ITT)
◆ Open University.

Teaching as a second career – mature entry

If you are 24 or over, you have the opportunity to combine 'real' teaching in IT with training which will ultimately lead to gaining a QTS award. This scheme is known as the licensed teacher scheme (LTS). It was designed mainly for mature entrants into the teaching profession, but is also available to non-graduate teachers who have trained overseas. Becoming a 'licensed teacher' gives you the chance to have some on-the-job training, similar to an apprenticeship. It is particularly useful when there is a shortage of qualified teachers in a certain area.

The main entry requirements for the licensed teacher scheme are:

◆ preferably hold a degree
◆ if no degree, must have two years' successful full-time higher education (or part-time equivalent)
◆ demonstrated a standard equivalent to GCSE grade C in English language and mathematics before your licence begins
◆ must be over 24 years old (unless you are a teacher trained overseas.

Priority subject recruitment scheme

In the summer of 1996 the Teacher Training Agency, realising the problems in attracting skilled professionals to the teaching profession, launched the priority recruitment scheme. The scheme operates by providing funds for individual teaching institutions (schools, colleges, universities) to make additional funds available so they can give monetary bonuses to those people who apply for teaching jobs in certain areas. Information technology is one of those areas, and anyone applying for a teaching position in IT will receive a bonus payment from the individual institutions which received the funding for the scheme. This bonus payment is in addition to the Local Education Authority (LEA) grant which is available.

If a career in education is what you are planning, it would be advisable to contact the teacher training institution(s) you are applying to in order to discuss their local arrangements.

Getting started

If you want to teach information technology as part of the National Curriculum, then it would be a good idea to have some understanding of what the National Curriculum is and how IT is to be taught within it.

All schools have copies of the National Curriculum and although it is unlikely that they will let you borrow them, they might let you have a look at them if you made an appointment. Alternatively, you can buy a copy of the National Curriculum, either as one complete book, or just the section relating to IT. A cheaper and probably more realistic option is to visit the library.

If you want to start doing a bit of general research into education and current IT teaching issues, it is worth reading the following papers. These papers also advertise vacancies in all levels of the educational system:

Monday: *The Times*
Tuesday: The *Guardian*
Thursday: The *Independent and* The *Daily Telegraph*
Friday: *Times Educational Supplement or 'TES'.*

Teachers' salary

School teachers' pay and conditions are regulated by the Department for Education and Employment. Recent pay awards have been between 2 and 3 per cent with higher increases at the lower end of the pay spine (the teachers' pay scale) for classroom teachers to encourage and improve the salaries of new entrants. Point 2 on the pay spine is the minimum starting salary for a newly qualified teacher with a good honours degree. As at June 1996, the salary range for classroom teachers was:

Pay Spine Level	Salary (£)
0	12,462
0.5	12,831
1	13,209
1.5	13,599
2	14,001
rising to...	
17	33,375

Where can I study for a teaching qualification?

For information on ITT courses (BEd, BSc + QTS and BA + QTS), consult the UCAS (Universities and Colleges Admissions Service) Handbook. UCAS handles all applications for university and college courses and it is essential reading for anyone intending to study at degree level. More information on the role of UCAS and contact details can be found in Chapter 11.

Contacts

For more information on teaching computing and IT in secondary schools, contact the Teacher Training Agency on 01245 454454 or write to:

The TTA Communication Centre, PO Box 3210, Chelmsford, Essex CM1 3WA.

For more information on postgraduate entry into teaching (PGCE courses), and an application form, contact the Graduate Teacher Training Registry on 01242 2258686 or write to:

Graduate Teacher Training Registry, Fulton House, Jessop Avenue, Cheltenham, Gloucestershire GL50 3SH.

For more information on the licensed teacher scheme, contact the Licensed Teacher Administration Unit on 01202 897691 or write to:

Licensed Teacher Administration Unit, Project Place, 1 Princes Road, Ferndown, Dorset BH22 9JG.

Working in a college or university

Teachers who work in further and higher education are normally referred to as lecturers and are paid on a slightly different pay scale to teachers. While you do not necessarily need a teaching qualification to become a college or university lecturer, you will almost certainly need a degree. A computing degree is preferred, but many other degrees are acceptable nowadays if they contain a suitable amount of IT-related subject material.

There is one main difference between working in a college (sixth-form or college of further education) and a university, and that is the emphasis placed on research. With funding constantly under threat, universities now need to establish close links with industry in order to obtain funding for new research programmes and new staff. One of the main ways universities obtain funding is by applying for research grants awarded by a number of scientific bodies in the European Union. As a result, many universities are now more interested in what research opportunities potential lecturers can bring to the university (and therefore, what money they can generate for the university), as opposed to their specific teaching skills. Competition is fierce for these positions; if you do want to become a university lecturer, you will ideally require:

♦ a good honours degree in an IT subject (preferably a 2:1 or first class)
♦ a higher degree (MSc, MPhil, PhD etc)
♦ specific research interests which match the university's own research programme.

Salary
Salaries for lecturers in colleges and universities vary enormously, depending on the institution, funding levels and local demand. Starting salaries for a graduate can be as low as £11,000, but if you already possess a few years' knowledge of industry or have a higher degree, salaries tend to be higher – around the £18,000 mark.

Getting started
To get an idea of the types of lectureships available throughout the

hundreds of colleges and universities in the UK, it is worth reading newspapers, such as *The Times Educational Supplement* as mentioned earlier.

Working in a university computer department

This vacancy for a job as a computer assistant, advertised during December 1996, explained the career opportunities working within a university computer services department extremely well:

Computer Assistant

Salary: £9,870 – £11,358

Role and responsibilities:
Working on the site's help desk, you will be the first point of contact for the computing support provided by University Computer Services Department. As this work involves a high degree of contact with students, you should have a pleasant and welcoming manner.
Main duties include:
● Help in resolution of users' problems
● Providing advice to users and identifying specialist support needs as required
● To assist in the preparation of documentation, enabling users to use installed software packages
● To assist with the installation and configuration of local computer and network equipment
● To assist with the investigation and correction of reported hardware and software faults and liaise with suppliers and departmental staff where necessary.

Personal skills required:
You should be able to communicate well – you will need to explain technical subjects clearly and frequently to inexperienced computer users. Experience in an advisory/help desk role would be advantageous.

Technical skills required:
A basic understanding of IT and MS-DOS/Windows is essential, as is experience of word-processing, spreadsheet and database

---

software (especially Microsoft product offerings). However, the ability to acquire new technical skills is also as important as those you already possess.

Qualifications:
Normally four GCSEs at ordinary level or equivalent plus appropriate keyboard skills and practical experience of computing equipment and software.

Research

Funded research

For those people who prefer to analyse and document new techniques in computing and IT rather than follow the normal route into commercial computing, a career in research is an obvious choice. Do not be misled into thinking the only way to achieve success in the IT profession is through the high-profile world of commercial computing, where salaries and benefit packages can seem irresistible.

Research is an exciting place for the IT professional, providing many opportunities to use and develop computer systems, often using state-of-the-art systems that would rarely be seen in the commercial sector. With investment returning to the IT world after some bleak periods, the opportunities for research have never been greater.

For most people, the two main routes into funded research are:

◆ studying for a degree by research
◆ applying for a salaried research post, usually in a university.

Degrees by research

Degrees by research are different from 'standard' postgraduate degrees, as they tend to be awarded purely on the result of a research project and the submission of a written thesis or dissertation. The main degrees which are offered for research purposes are MPhil and DPhil or PhD, although some institutions do offer an

MSc by research. If you intend applying for one of these degrees, you will almost certainly need a very good first degree in computing or a closely related discipline. Research students for whom the research for a degree is their main activity are funded by a grant (known as a bursary), which is usually in the region of £5,000. Competition is fierce for research places, especially for the few funded research studentships which are offered by some of the universities, providing the student with extra funding during their degree.

Salaried research

If you want to assist in the research for an IT-related project in a university, usually funded by one of the European research bodies, you can apply for a post as a research assistant, which carries a salary. Again, for this post you will need a very good computing degree, and possibly even a higher degree as well (such as an MSc or PhD). Although research assistants often work on their own initiative, they are usually supervised by a research director who will provide guidance and direction during their research. Typical salaries for a research assistant are between £14,000 and £20,000.

--- **Case Study** ---

Richard *is a computer studies lecturer*

'After joining the IT industry as a computing graduate, I soon realised that I was not using and developing my interpersonal skills as much as I would have liked. I've always enjoyed talking about IT issues as much as I have enjoyed the technical side of the job, so it was only a matter of time before I started to look for a job in the teaching profession (although I knew very little about it at the time). If I had one worry, it was that I might end up becoming something out of 'Grange Hill' – losing all my computing skills but being a dab-hand with the blackboard!

Finding a suitable job was relatively easy, as the majority of vacancies for college lecturers appeared in *The Times Educational Supplement*, which I bought every week. I think my experience of industry helped me a lot in my interview (which included the principal of the college and various heads of department) as the college was keen to keep up-to-date with the 'real world' of IT. Coming straight from industry, the college also booked me on a City & Guilds course to learn the basics of teaching in further education before I started my first term, which was really helpful.

I have a wide and varied programme of courses to teach, ranging from short one-day courses on computer programming to HND-level Systems Analysis and Design. Funding is a problem at the moment though, and so I have to teach an evening class, just until the college can afford a part-time lecturer to ease my workload. Of course, I also have non-teaching responsibilities; I also provide a 'pastoral' role for my students, and I do make time for them should they wish to discuss their problems with me – whatever they are; a responsibility which I take very seriously.'

5 Occupations within computing and information technology

Most companies which use IT usually have a separate department from which all the organisation's IT activities can be managed . Of course, there are bound to be slight differences in the overall structure of IT departments, but most will be similar in structure to Figure 5.1. Typically, IT departments tend to be structured around the various functions the department must perform as a whole, such as development and support. It is worth spending some time at this stage to consider what area of work appeals to you: support or development would be an obvious choice, but then again, you may want to go straight into a sales or marketing role.

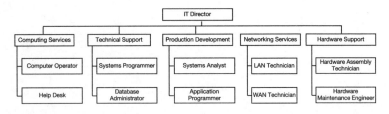

Figure 5.1 *The structure of a typical commercial IT department*

Within this chapter, I've tried to provide as much relevant information as possible for each of the areas discussed, but remember, all companies have a slightly different approach to IT, so this information can only be general in nature. The individual case studies in this chapter are, however, specific to individuals who have had first-hand experience of working within the IT industry.

Treat these as 'insider knowledge' from people who have been successful in their own career development. If you need a source of inspiration to get your IT career started, consider these case studies as your guiding light.

Computing services

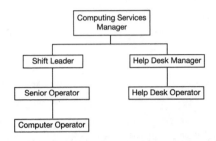

Figure 5.2 *The Computing Services team structure*

The computer operator

Over the years, the role of the computer operator has changed significantly and is now often one of the most dynamic within the IT department. Computer operators perform an important function as they are the people who provide first-line support for the computer system, often 24 hours a day, every day of the year. Not only do they keep the system working 'normally', ie within agreed limits of availability (9am–5pm for instance), they are also expected to investigate any problems on the computer system and take the appropriate action to fix it. If they cannot fix the problem, they pass it on to the next line of support (second-line support), which will mean a call to one or more of the support teams, such as the systems programmers or network technicians. Traditionally, computer operators worked almost exclusively on mainframe platforms; the role of today's computer operator is often much different. Due to the 'client-server' design of many computer systems, computer operators must manage any number of different computer platforms and operating systems (such as MVS, UNIX, AS/400) which may be connected over large telecommunications networks.

Main Tasks

◆ Making system backups on to computer tape.
◆ Scheduling daily, weekly and monthly work on the computer, eg monthly payroll applications.
◆ Loading computer tapes into tape drives for processing.
◆ Ensuring user applications have been started and stopped at the correct times.
◆ Producing statistics on the performance of the computer.
◆ Identifying and resolving computer system errors.
◆ Providing general support for the computer system and the applications running on it.

Many computer operators are required to work shift patterns to ensure the computer system is available every day of the year. While this may not suit everyone, many operators enjoy shift work, especially the bonus payments which they get for being on shift on top of their normal salary (often in the region of 33 per cent).

Salary

Trainee computer operator: £9,000 upwards. Computer operator: £10,000 – £20,000

Case Study

John is an Operations Shift Leader.

'When I left school at 16, I wasn't really sure what I wanted to do, although I knew I had more than an interest in computing. On the qualifications front, I did have maths and computing O-levels, so I applied for a job in the operations department of a local manufacturer. When I arrived for my first day of work, I was pleasantly surprised to find that no one in the operations team had a degree, as I'd thought it would be essential for this sort of job

I soon realised why – the type of work we did was specific to our computer – an IBM mainframe, and a degree would have been of no immediate benefit to the team. After a few months and a fair amount of on-the-job training, I was soon performing all the duties expected of an operator, such as re-running batch jobs which had failed during the overnight schedule and diagnosing networking problems (we have a high-speed fibre-optic link between ourselves and one of our major suppliers).

After two enjoyable years as a computer operator, I moved jobs and I am now an Operations Shift Leader with one of the privatised utility companies. As you would expect, their computer department is huge, and the operations department have first-line responsibility for IBM mainframes, IBM Unix servers and an IBM AS/400. Although I still have operating duties, being a shift leader means I am also responsible for the four other operators in my shift as well as the computer systems. When things go wrong, people turn to me to determine what has gone wrong and to fix it as quickly as possible.

While there are many people who see working in operations as the starting place for other careers in IT, such as systems programming, I am quite happy where I am; I'm in a management position, yet I'm learning new technical skills all the time, such as UNIX and Oracle. What more could I ask for?'

The help desk operator

The help desk is usually a small department often working within the computer operations area providing a customer-friendly 'first-line' support role. Unlike the computer operators, staff working on the help desk provide general help and advice to all the users of the computer system. Working with business users as opposed to technical staff, the help desk operator provides the important link between the non-technical user and the computer technical support staff.

Skills required:

◆ Patience and understanding (not everyone is computer-literate!)

◆ Pleasing manner (by the time many users have contacted the help desk, they will have gone mad trying to get their system to work and they will probably take it out on you!)

◆ General understanding of how computer systems work (many 'users' are quite happy to talk about LANs, WANs, CPU, disk drives etc, are you?)

While some help desk operators are highly skilled computer technicians, often resolving lengthy and complex user problems, the average help desk operator would perform tasks relating to:

- logging of user problems on the help desk problem database
- trying to resolve day-to-day problems (such as users forgetting their system password)
- making users aware of any major work taking place on the computer system that might prevent them from using it
- passing more complex problems to the support teams for fixing
- contacting computer manufacturers and suppliers to place service calls with them if an error is identified with one of their products.

Salary
Help desk operator: £7,000 – £15,000. Technical Help Desk Operator: £10,000 – £20,000.

Production development

Figure 5.3 *The Production Development team structure*

The systems analyst

The role of the systems analyst is often seen as one of the most challenging within the IT industry, as it is the systems analyst who must initially convert a business requirement (eg 'we need a better order-processing system') into a series of functional stages which other IT professionals such as computer programmers and database designers will understand.

Historically, systems analysts had a specific role within data-processing, or DP departments as they sometimes called. Having clear boundaries within which to work, when they had completed their investigations, they would pass their specifications for the proposed computer system to the application programming team.

Nowadays, the boundaries in many IT departments have changed, and systems analysts can find themselves performing many other roles previously performed by other IT staff, such as programming and testing.

Once an IT project has been started, usually with the publication of a proposal document, the systems analyst must begin to understand the customer's current system (regardless of whether it is implemented on a computer or not) in order to become fully aware of their business functions and procedures.

It is important that the systems analyst focuses closely on the users' requirements throughout the project and what they are expecting to be delivered at the end of the project – any misunderstandings by the user or the analyst could seriously impact the success of the project. To help prevent this happening, the systems analyst will refer to a document produced at the start of the project, the 'Terms of reference', which will identify the objectives and the scope of the project, and clarify exactly what is expected by the customer and when the completed system will be delivered to them.

While there are many different types of analyst within the IT industry, they will all perform a similar set of tasks during the lifecycle of an IT project. Here are the main tasks an analyst will be expected to perform:

Feasibility study

Before any development work takes place, the systems analyst must investigate the customer's requirements carefully and decide whether it is possible to design an IT system which can meet those requirements. To do this, the systems analyst must perform an intensive information-gathering exercise, talking to customers, users, managers – anyone in fact who is involved with the current system. The reasoning is simple: before you can design computer applications, you must first understand what they are expected to perform and why. Questions the systems analyst might ask a business user during this stage of a project might be something like:

why do you perform that task? Where do you log new customer details? What happens after the invoice has been received?

As well as investigating the current system, the systems analyst must also identify the requirements of the new computer system – for instance, there might be a new business function which needs incorporating into the existing system.

Design specification

During this phase of a project, the systems analyst will document how the proposed system will be designed; in other words, what business procedures and functions must exist in the solution for it to meet the customer's requirements. For example, if the customer wanted to computerise their stock-control system, some of the business procedures and functions would include checking current stock levels, searching for stock details and ordering new stock. It is from these specifications that the application programmers can develop the new computer system – a business function or procedure in the specification will relate to some form of computer program in the solution. In smaller companies, the analyst will not only produce the specification for the application programs required, but will also undertake the programming tasks. This joint role of analyst/programmer is becoming more and more widespread as many IT companies now require staff with a mixture of programming and analytical skills. Depending on the size of the design team, and the nature of the project, the analyst may also produce specifications for other parts of the system, such as the database which will store all the stock details in the previous example. With computer systems now becoming split up over different company sites ('distributed computer systems'), the analyst must decide the best way of storing and accessing the data. At all times the main focus is on the customer – they will have to use the system.

Main skills

The role of a systems analyst is often a complex one, combining many different technical and managerial skills. As much of their work involves gathering and collating information from users as well as the technical design tasks, you will find that most systems analysts possess the following skills:

◆ Clear and logical approach to problem solving (can you ask the right questions?)
◆ Good verbal communication (can you write and speak clearly, enabling people to understand you?)
◆ Customer-facing (IT-jargon for being well-presented and professional when dealing with customers)
◆ Data modelling/diagrammatic representation (can you produce clear, understandable diagrams which model the customer's current and proposed systems?)
◆ Business awareness (can you appreciate the customer's problem from a business perspective? Are you able to identify important business risks as well as benefits?)

After looking at this demanding list of skills, you can understand why many systems analysts have performed other IT roles, such as programming or support before moving into analysis. Systems analysis is not an easy role in IT for the inexperienced starter – even if that person is a graduate.

Salary
A graduate systems analyst can expect to earn anything between £15,000 and £20,000 a year. With experience, systems analysts (or business consultants) can easily attract salaries in the region of £30,000–£50,000 a year.

Case Study

Clare *is a business systems analyst.*

'In 1987 I graduated from university with a degree in Business Studies, with the intention of being in management by the time I was 30. I'm pleased to say that didn't happen as I'm now thoroughly enjoying my current career as a business systems analyst with a major manufacturing company, based in London. I joined the company's graduate recruitment scheme as a graduate trainee, and became a trainee analyst by the time the programme had been completed. For the next two years I assisted in several small analysis projects, working in a small team. Although I found it interesting, I also found it difficult at first, especially when it came to modelling business systems with diagrams such as entity-relationship-diagrams and dataflow diagrams. I think my business degree did help me in the early stages, as understanding the business and the user requirements is vital for this sort of work.

Gaining promotion to an analyst, for the next four years I performed the role of lead analyst in a support environment. During that time I was responsible for documenting user requirements and producing and updating system specifications which I passed to the programming team to code. I am now a systems analyst which means I am responsible for the whole process of requirements analysis, producing functional and system specifications and terms of reference within my section. I now have to justify my decisions to the IT manager, so I have just been sent on a cost-benefit analysis course to help me. It's a demanding job; a mistake so early on in a project could put the 'cat amongst the pigeons'! In my current position, I get the chance to meet lots of people and perform my objectives with very little supervision, which is what I like. In many ways, I am responsible for many of my actions, but having been in an analysis role since joining the company, I've got a good idea how things are done!'

The application programmer

Application development is the largest occupational area within IT for very good reasons – it is through application software that most benefit is gained for the users of information technology. Application programmers historically wrote the majority of business applications in languages such as COBOL and PL/1 on mainframe computers, and although there are still opportunities in these areas, a lot of development work is now performed with PC-based software packages.

Popular software packages for application development, such as Visual Basic, Visual C++ and Oracle, provide the application programmer with a large number of development 'tools' to help them reduce the amount of coding they need to perform. These save the programmer a great deal of time in not having to write many software routines to perform functions which will be needed many times during the development of the program. Such is the ease and speed in writing computer applications with these software packages, they are often used in new techniques to application development called RAD (Rapid Application Development). RAD allows the programmer (or analyst/programmer) to develop prototypes of the proposed application, including any new application screens the customer needs, very quickly. This is one of the main benefits with using RAD tools: the application programmer can show the prototype to the customer before any major development work takes place. If there are any slight modifications needed, these can be easily changed at this stage without affecting the overall system development process.

Main tasks

Whatever method of application development is used, the tasks for the programmer remain the same:

◆ Design the computer program using a series of 'English-like' statements which document the logical way of solving the problem eg,
for each customer in customer file
read account file
if customer's balance = 0
then write 'Customer balance is zero' in customer file.

◆ Write the application code using the most appropriate programming language or software package available. The program generated may be a brand new program or, more commonly, a modification to an existing program.

◆ Test the program to ensure there are no errors within it (or 'bugs' as they are known). This will often involve using a test computer system which is an exact copy of the current production system.

◆ Document the computer program so it can be maintained and modified at a later date. It is often the case that the person who has to maintain a computer program is not the person who wrote it – many programs are passed over to the application support teams when they have been written, freeing up the original programmer to work on a different project.

To be a programmer you need to have a clear and logical mind as you will need to develop a programming solution to whatever business problem you are confronted with; and of course, the better you are at designing programs, the easier you will find it to move from using one programming language to another. For instance, many of the mainframe COBOL programmers of the 1980s are now happily programming in Visual Basic and Oracle.

Main skills

◆ Able to reason logically (try completing the popular 'logic puzzle' magazines!)

◆ Able to work with a problem generating alternative solutions (not every solution will be the most effective – it could cause other problems).

◆ Able to provide clear, understandable and well-structured program code (someone else may have to make modifications to your program later).

◆ Able to produce solutions which match customer requirements (you might think it is a great piece of code – but does it do the job correctly?)

Application programmers usually work in teams, with the team leader performing a combined role of programming and management. Within the team there will probably be a number of experienced application programmers and a small number of junior programmers. While they will all write application code, it is likely that the experienced programmers will design and write the main functional routines in the program on which the rest of the application code will depend. Junior programmers will often write smaller and less crucial parts of the application and perform other tasks such as writing the documentation and testing the program.

Salary

Junior programmers: £9,000 upwards. Computing graduates: £12,000–£20,000.

Case Study

Diane *is a mainframe application programmer.*

'Originally, the idea of entering the computer profession was not one of my career aims, which is why I decided to study for a degree in English language. On graduating, I realised that I did not really want to become an English teacher, so, realising that IT was going to be with us for some time, I decided to study for an MSc conversion course in Information technology. The course allowed graduates in one discipline to grasp the basics of another subject within a year – it was an intensive course, but well worth the many hours I spent in the computer labs. I found this course really interesting, and I even managed to use some of my English skills when we studied artificial intelligence and natural language processing (getting computers to understand speech).

Feeling more confident with IT, I joined Rolls Royce as I wanted to work for a large company which had a graduate training programme. Within six months of joining I had learnt the basics of programming in PL/1, which is a 'high-level' language used for business computing. I soon realised the importance of writing 'structured' programs, as it not only makes them easier to design and write, but also much easier for other people to maintain as well. After 'graduating' from the computer training centre, I started to use my new skills in a small project team based in the computer building. At first, I was just writing the odd line here and there – basically amending other people's programs to perform slightly better, but not long after, I was writing complex programs myself.

At times, I find it hard to believe how far I've progressed in the IT world, when I could so easily have joined the teaching profession. I've now moved into a senior programming position with a major catering company and I'm currently learning how to program in Visual Basic so I can start to write new applications for the catering staff who use PCs in the various company sites.'

Technical support

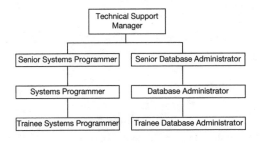

Figure 5.4 *The Technical Support team structure*

The systems programmer

Within any computer system, there are a number of special files and applications which are required by the computer system itself. These files are collectively termed 'systems software' and maintaining them is one of the many tasks performed by the systems programmer.

The systems programmer will often have to use programming instructions and commands which are run directly against the computer's operating system. With any commands which change part of the computer system, there is a risk that they might cause major problems as a result, which is why some of these tasks are sometimes performed at weekends when the computer system will not be required by the business users.

Main tasks

♦ Installing new versions of computer software (applications or operating system).
♦ Fixing system-level errors on the computer.
♦ Configuring systems software, eg data backup utilities.
♦ Carrying out system performance and tuning tasks.
♦ Controlling access and security to the computer system software.
♦ Providing general second-line support services for the computer system users

Salary

Trainee systems programmers: £12,000–£15,000. Graduate systems programmers: £12,000–£20,000.

Case Study

Chris *is a mainframe systems programmer.*

'I did a three year BSc chemistry course at Surrey University. I obtained a summer job with an ICI research station where I found that a PhD was the minimum requirement to make any reasonable progress in the chemical industry. I therefore decided to get a job in the computer industry, another interest of mine.

I joined Datasolve as graduate trainee in the operations department. This gave me a good grounding in how a commercial computer system is put together. I progressed to running a shift of 12 staff running multiple machines across multiple sites and performed a wide range of tasks in many different areas, including console operations, data communications, tape handling, printing and disaster recovery.

I moved out of operations into mainframe automation first with Datasolve and later with the Post Office. My operations experience was essential, enabling me to program the computer systems to perform the required actions. Automation mainly consists of determining the most appropriate actions (rather than those currently being carried out) and then configuring the system software to perform them. Recently I have become involved in a large project to automate and integrate all the other computer platforms used within the business.

I have found my scientific training useful for analysing operational requirements and writing various reports in a clear, objective manner. My operations experience has proved invaluable, and has given me an in-depth understanding of how the various components of a complex computer environment fit together.'

The database administrator

Many business applications access large amounts of information which are stored as a single logical structure; a database in other words. While there are many different database systems used within the IT industry, such as IBM's DB2 and Oracle, they all share one main characteristic – they all contain *related* items of data. Business information which needs adding to the database is usually entered by special computer programs called 'transactions', which allow the user to enter data from their own computer terminal. A typical transaction performed by a user would be to add, modify or delete information stored in the database – a stock record for instance.

As you can imagine, over time, as more users run transactions against the database, it will gradually increase in size and if left unmanaged will eventually cause problems. It is vitally important that the structure of the database and the complex relationships of the data within it are maintained regularly, otherwise inconsistencies in the data could occur. This is a highly technical process and can only be performed by a skilled technician who knows exactly how the database has been designed and implemented on the computer system – the database administrator.

Main tasks

◆ Maintaining the integrity of the data within the database (are the data valid and accurate?)

◆ Ensuring the database can be recovered in the event of an error (eg computer crash, corruption due to a 'virus', power failure).

◆ Tuning the database (will the database still perform well when more data are added to it?)

◆ Sizing the database (how large will it need to be if we add another two hundred users onto the computer system?)

Salary

Trainee database administrators: £12,000–£15,000. Graduate database administrators: £12,000–£20,000

Case Study

John *is a mainframe database administrator.*

'When I was at school all those years ago I was not very academic and, leaving school with very few qualifications, ended up working in the mail room of our local sweet factory. I can remember it well, it was very boring and routine. This all changed when the company had a mainframe computer installed some years later. Wanting a change from sorting mail and parcels, I applied for a position as a trainee computer operator in the computer room. I got it, but I didn't get away from sorting paper, as my first task was to keep the huge printers stocked up with continuous paper all day.

Eventually, I became a computer operator, and after a few more years' experience and attending a few technical courses, I became an MVS systems programmer. Having been in the company all my working life, my role became quite easy, to be honest, as I understood all the user applications and how they ran on the mainframe computer. However, the company was growing faster than the computer system, so the company decided to install IBM's relational database management system (DB2), to store all the company stock and price information. This was about the biggest project the company had ever tackled since the installation of the mainframe computer and while it was exciting to be part of an IBM project, I was a bit nervous as I had been asked to install the database system software on the mainframe! The company sent me on an IBM course in London to install and configure DB2 which lasted a week, by which time I was confident in what I had to do back at work. The project went very well, and I was promoted to database administrator within the computer department – the first one ever. To be honest, things were hectic at first and I ended up working quite a few weekends to tune the database parameters as it was the only time I could get to close the database down without affecting the users. I'm glad to say the system is working fine now, requiring very little maintenance, which has allowed me time to get involved with the next database project which involves working with UNIX – something I've never used before! I'm excited at the prospect of gaining new skills, and I know my mainframe DB2 experience will help me understand many of the database issues on the new system.'

Networking services

Figure 5.5 *The Networking Services team structure*

The LAN technician

Over the last few years, the users of computing and information technology have witnessed a phenomenal rise in the number of computer networks used within the organisation. Many departments now need to share business information with other users within the organisation; they can do this by using one or more LANs linking many business users together.

Many LANs are now either PC-based or UNIX-based due to their networking and graphics capabilities, and it is within this area the LAN technician becomes involved. The LAN technician must be able to design suitable networks so that everyone who needs access to the information can get it. This is not as simple as it sounds, especially when you might have to connect different types of computers on different types of LAN.

Main tasks

◆ Connecting computers to LAN networks, on mainframe, midrange or desktop platforms.

◆ Designing and building networks using technologies such as Ethernet and Token Ring.

◆ Configuring network software to add new connections or restrict access to certain users on the network.

◆ Identifying and resolving errors on the network (eg congestion and slow response).

Main skills

◆ Knowledge of LAN software, such as Novell Netware on PCs, LAN Manager for UNIX systems and TCP/IP (Transmission Control Protocol/Internet Protocol – a networking protocol popular in UNIX networks and on the Internet).

◆ Knowledge of LAN networking hardware, such as PC-networking cards, token-ring adapters and hubs.

Salary

LAN technician: £9,000–£15,000. Graduates with networking experience: £12,000–£20,000.

Case Study

Mike *is a network technician responsible for a number of departmental LANs.*

'Having spent five years programming with a large retail chain, I was never really interested in networking at first. Like most of my colleagues, I did not really appreciate networking, and I suppose I just saw it as messing around with lots of cables and switches. My opinion soon changed when the company expanded its mainframe computer system to incorporate UNIX and PC systems. All of a sudden, the network became something we could all associate with, as we all started having Ethernet cards slotted in our PCs and we were all given IP addresses showing our unique address on the network. I realised that working in the network team could be an exciting move for me, and I haven't looked back since. The company sent me on a few basic courses to learn about the major protocols used on the network – TCP/IP and SNMP – and within a few weeks the whole fuzzy area of networking became clear!

The networking team are now looking into development of the Internet, fire-walls (a UNIX server which protects the rest of the network against unauthorised access) and lots of other exciting new developments which are happening within the IT and networking world. As the IT department is constantly expanding its PC LAN, I'm hoping I can learn more about Novell Netware, and maybe gain CNE certification in the future. With this qualification, I will be able to help design and configure all the future LANs within the department – quite an achievement for an ex-COBOL programmer!'

The WAN technician

The term 'wide area network' applies to any type of computer network which covers a large physical area. Typically WANs are used to transfer information between companies in different geographical locations, either within the same country, or worldwide. These sorts of communications system are extremely complex, requiring not only an understanding of networking equipment such as bridges, routers and network controllers, but also of the telecommunications systems used to relay the data, such as high-speed digital telephone lines or satellite communications. The WAN technician will often work closely with telecommunications companies and networking hardware suppliers in order to build data networks using public or private telephone lines across the country. Sometimes, the backbone network will already be in place, which means extra users can be added on to it by the addition of a piece of networking hardware – sometimes that whole 'branch' of the network will need to be added. Once the WAN has been installed, a lot of time will be spent monitoring and tuning the network, which could be routing data between many towns and cities, even countries, all the time. As you can imagine with such a widespread system containing many 'connections', the scope for error is quite high. Not only that, but the WAN technician must identify faults on the network which might have been caused by a failing network component hundreds of miles away!

Main tasks

◆ To install (or commission a network or telecommunications supplier to install) network hardware and attach it to the telecommunications links.

◆ To install software to monitor and configure the network (such as reporting errors in connection or high usage which may cause response-time problems).

◆ To document the company's network structure in order to help manage and expand the network (maybe using PC-based network modelling tools).

◆ To build any 'test' networks which might be needed by the organisation.

Main Skills

◆ Knowledge of WAN technologies used in data transfer, such as X25, IBM's SNA (Systems Network Architecture), TCP/IP and ATM (Asynchronous Transfer Method).

◆ Knowledge of WAN networking hardware (modems, multiplexers, network controllers, bridges, gateways and routers).

Salary

WAN technician: £9,000–£15,000. Graduates with networking experience: £12,000–£20,000.

Hardware support

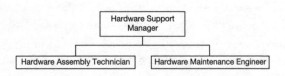

Figure 5.6 *The Hardware Support team structure*

The hardware assembly technician

Many new computer systems are custom-built to user requirements, and it is the job of the hardware assembly technician to assemble and test such systems. This type of work typically involves building computers, such as PCs, by 'plugging' together a number of required components such as disk drives, power supplies, circuit boards and cooling systems. Obviously, for this sort of role an interest in electronics is useful as well as a general understanding of computers. Generally, a degree is not required for this role, as many companies will take on school-leavers with GCSEs and provide training.

Salary
Hardware assembly technician/hardware test engineer: £9,000–£15,000.

The hardware maintenance engineer

Computer equipment, just like any other electronic equipment, is bound to fail sometime during its life span. While the average household could survive a day or two without the TV or washing machine, the average company would start to lose money if vital computer equipment was not fixed as soon as possible. The hardware maintenance engineer therefore plays an important role in keeping the computer hardware systems working correctly by providing such services as:

◆ either replacing or repairing faulty computer equipment
◆ performing diagnostics on devices suspected of being faulty (usually by running diagnostic computer software which identifies faults and recommended solutions)
◆ installing and testing new computer hardware.

All of the major computer suppliers have their own hardware engineers who provide service and support for customers in their local area, so a fair amount of travel can be involved in shipping parts to customers and installing them at their computer site. While a good understanding of electronics and computer hardware is expected for this role, a degree is not necessary as vendor-specific courses are often preferred to general hardware skills – ie if you are supporting IBM computer hardware, you would attend an IBM hardware course.

Salary
Hardware maintenance engineer: £9,000–£20,000.

Freelance IT contractors

All of the major reports on employment opportunities commissioned by the IT industry predict there will be a huge rise in the number of contract staff. While this is no great surprise, it does reflect the changing values of both employees and employers within the IT industry. Flexibility is the key to being a contractor, and while you must be willing to work anywhere, for anyone on any project, you can expect to be rewarded well for your efforts.

Most contractors work for themselves in the sense that they own their own company, into which their salary is paid by the company they work for. While the idea of being the managing director of your own company may sound an exciting prospect, it does have its drawbacks. For one thing, you will have to pay National Insurance contributions both as an employee *and* an employer. You will also have to pay for any training you require (unless you can make 'an arrangement' with your employer) and lose your entitlement to company sick pay.

Contractors are required in all the major areas of IT support and development for all sorts of reasons – the main one being to source a short-term skills requirement on a major project. For this reason, most contracts are between three and six months' duration, but contracts of 12 months are now becoming more common as well. Hundreds of jobs for contractors are advertised every week in *Computing* and *Computer Weekly*, but there are a number of IT magazines specifically aimed at those working as contractors, such as *Freelance Informer*.

For more information on contract opportunities, contact the following trade magazines for details of subscription (you might be eligible for a free subscription if you already work in the IT profession).

Computing/Computer Contractor VNU Business Publications, The Circulation Manager, VNU House, 32–4 Broadwick Street, London W1A 2HG; 0171 316 9000

Computer Weekly/Freelance Informer
Reed Business Publishing, Circulation Manager, Quadrant House, The Quadrant, Sutton, Surrey SM2 5AS: 01444 441212.

Freelance Informer helpline: 01622 778222

Salary
On average, a freelance IT contractor can expect to earn £1,000 a week. Well-paid contracts for skills in demand can attract salaries of £2,000 a week.

Case Study

Dave *is a freelance computer contractor.*

'As far as qualifications go with regard to computers when I left school, I had none. Although I did do O-level computer studies and was top of the class, everybody failed the exam, including myself.

Armed with only three O-levels in maths, physics and biology, my career aim of computers was way off target. However, I was lucky and I managed to get on the YTS (Youth Training Scheme) to become an office trainee.

I was at the YTS for just under four months before I was offered a job as computer operator at the local council offices, so at 18 my computer career began. I had hit my target, even though I had to do shift work. I stayed with the council for about two years, gaining experience with mainframe computers.

My career really took off with my next job. Again with mainframes, but with a more technical involvement. Excelling at programming and job correction, I was promoted through the ranks of operator, senior operator and then shift leader quite quickly. Here I began to teach myself the COBOL programming language – if you want to get somewhere you have to motivate yourself, no one is going to give it to you.

I left the company after two and a half years, only months before it folded, and moved into the realms of technical support with a different company – no more shift work like before and my programming skills came in handy. However, it was a larger company and the technical involvement was limited.

Accepting my next job after two and a half years was another career turn. A smaller company, but the technical exposure was enormous. Here, I was exposed to UNIX and I wanted to get involved, but was initially rejected, so I put myself on a weekend UNIX training course and a City & Guilds 'C' programming language course in the evenings – which I passed. I think I proved something to the company, and with that, I became involved with UNIX.

After two years with the company I was made redundant, but was asked to stay around during the handover period while the FM company got to grips with the company's computer systems.

Being unemployed was not fun; however, it gave me the chance to revise my skills and to look into something that I had been thinking about for some time – contracting. Maybe being made redundant had been a blessing in disguise. After two months' redundancy, I had my first contract with my own company in the UNIX market. My career now has rocket boosters attached. I can now obtain more training by putting myself on more courses and gain more skills to make myself more marketable.

I haven't looked back since.'

Occupations outside the IT department

Computer sales

In some ways, being in computer sales is one of the most important roles within the IT profession, and it is probably one of the best paid too, for that matter. Computer sales staff provide business with the computer hardware and software they need to solve their problems and increase profitability. While sales staff have a wide knowledge of computer systems, they will often rely on specialist technicians to provide specific answers to specific business problems, both before and after the sale – pre-sales support staff and post-sales support staff. A good knowledge of business, often in a specific field, such as retail or personnel systems is essential, as is a shrewd mind for figures. While salaries for sales staff are usually high, part of their salary is normally in the form of a commission, based on the value of the contract. Most of the top sales staff are graduates, who can combine their technical expertise with management skills they have developed. However, there are opportunities for people from technical backgrounds to move into sales, maybe after performing a marketing or pre-sales support role first.

Salary

Salaries in sales can vary enormously due to commission. An average salary would be in the region of £20,000–£50,000, but salaries of £250,000 are attainable in some of the large IT companies.

Case Study

Angela *works in the sales department for a major systems software company.*

'Although I'm in sales, my official job title is account manager – it's a bit more customer friendly than salesman (or saleswoman), which is often the first step to getting a sale! Working for a large software house whose products are specifically designed to help IBM mainframe computer centre support staff, I don't really need to 'sell' products as such – technical support managers tend to come to me first with their problems! In my business I deal with the customer all the time, either the technical support manager, or sometimes the IT director. Whatever, they will have a clear picture of what they need from me, although they might not be aware of our latest piece of software which might help them. This is why I tend to bring a few technical specialists with me after the initial meeting, so they can demonstrate the product and answer any specific queries which the customer may have (apart from 'How much does it cost?' – that's my job). I do understand the basics of the products from a technical point of view as I started off as a computer programmer and then spent a few years as a team leader in a technical support environment before I eventually moved into sales.

The job is very demanding; I have to travel a lot and meet customers at their convenience, not mine – so if that means meeting them at 7pm on a Friday, then that's when I've got to go. Luckily, I enjoy meeting people and having a good chat about their specific requirements and what they've been up to recently – it all helps build rapport with the customer. The only down-side is that the business lunches tend to play havoc with my figure! If I could sum up my role in one sentence, I would say 'hard work, but full of perks!'

Technical author

It is the job of the technical author to design and produce technical publications and documents which will be required by people using computer systems. You might think that this task would be performed by the technical support and development staff; in some smaller companies this is probably true, but in larger companies there are usually specialists in this area to perform this task A typical situation a technical author might encounter is being asked to write documentation such as:

◆ user guides (for people new to the computer application)
◆ technical reference manuals (for technicians who must support the computer systems)
◆ technical magazines, flysheets and any other form of written communication which requires technical information.

A technical author needs a rare set of skills, combining the roles of author and publisher with those of a technician. While word-processing packages are widely used within the IT industry, a technical author will often use more sophisticated document-composition software, such as that used within the electronic publishing profession.

Salary
Starting salaries tend to fall in the range £8,000–£15,000.

IT Trainer

With the phenomenal growth in the use and development of IT systems, the role of the trainer is becoming ever more important. As more and more businesses begin to use and develop IT hardware and software, so there is an increasing need for staff to be trained to use such systems. Not surprisingly, IT training is currently an area which is expanding at a particularly high rate compared to other occupational areas within the IT industry. Training can cover all sorts of systems, packages and computer systems, and ranges from teaching a small group of people a few simple instructions on a PC to providing classroom-based training for a whole department on the use of a new software product.

The most important skill required for an IT trainer is to be able to communicate often complex ideas simply. Basically, you must be *understood*. Obviously, you will be required to possess good technical skills as well, usually in one or two main areas and maybe general IT skills in other areas. It is worth remembering that you will often be stood in front of people most of the time during a normal day, either explaining the subject to them or helping them solve any problems they might be experiencing – you will need to remain calm, patient and, above all, professional at all times. Not an easy job, especially when your authority might be challenged by one of the smarter pupils in your class!

Most companies are prepared to take on A-level candidates as well as graduates, usually into some form of 'train the trainers' programme.

Salary

Starting salaries vary greatly in this area, from £10,000 for the more junior positions, to around £20,000 for graduates with experience.

Case Study

Michelle *is a freelance trainer.*

'Having worked for a number of years as a systems programmer in the early days of the UNIX operating system, I realised that I actually enjoyed telling people how the computer system worked. I suspect this is partly due to the fact that I do like meeting people and I consider myself to be a good communicator, especially on technical issues. For the next two years I worked in the training department of the computer vendor I worked for and enjoyed myself immensely. Not only did I have to provide a technical role in planning the course structure and content, but I also had to manage the external contractors we employed for specific courses.

Recognising the increasing demand for IT trainers, I then started contracting, giving me the freedom to train people from many different companies. Working in the M4 corridor, I am now employed by a number of major computer vendors who use freelance contractors, such as Hewlett-Packard and Sun Microsystems. The work is varied, and I do get a lot of free time between courses, which is quite nice in the demanding world of IT. If I had a dislike in being a trainer, it would be the amount of travelling I can sometimes end up doing between customer sites – still, my salary more than makes up for that!'

---

6   Getting started

While this book has highlighted some of the many exciting career opportunities within the IT profession, it does not necessarily mean you will be offered the first job that you apply for. True, there is currently a severe skills shortage affecting the IT industry, but that is no guarantee that the skills you have are those required by an employer. To be successful in achieving your career aims, you must plan: start by thinking about where you want to be in a few years' time and how you are going to get there. Hopefully, you will have already started doing a bit of planning (you are, after all, reading a book which will help you). Consider these questions as 'checkpoints' in your planning:

◆ What area of IT would you like to work in? (Supplier, VAR, IT user, education etc.)
◆ What job role suits your current skills best?
◆ What job role would you *prefer* if you had the choice?
◆ Where do you want to be in one/three/five years' time?
◆ Do you need to gain new skills first?
◆ Do you want to specialise in a particular field?
◆ Do you want to start work with minimal qualifications and gain experience?
◆ Do you want to study for a degree first and then think about what you want to do?
◆ Where do you want to work (locally, anywhere in the UK, anywhere in the world)?

Armed with this information, you can now decide how to make

your first move to help you get a job in IT. You could decide to defer writing job applications until you have gained specific skills or qualifications, or you could decide to enter the profession straight away.

Finding a job

With the current skills shortage in IT, the number of advertised positions easily exceeds the number of people capable of filling them. Unfortunately, vacancies in the IT industry do not make headline news, so it is important you know where to look to find that job vacancy with your name on it.

There are a number of sources where computing and IT jobs are regularly advertised; below is a list of the main sources of information for IT job-hunters, but it is not a definitive list – you must also act on your own initiative:

◆ local and national newspapers
◆ job-seekers' newspapers
◆ IT trade magazines
◆ Job Centres
◆ university/college careers service
◆ Channel 4 Teletext page 641
◆ the Internet
◆ computer recruitment fairs.

It is said that many IT jobs are never advertised. Why? Well, one of the main reasons is because they have been filled on the basis of personal recommendation, or someone simply 'being in the right place at the right time'. Unfortunately, the IT industry is no different to any other in that respect, so it is important to remain focused and determined on the task ahead. Whatever job you do apply for, you can be sure of one thing – many others will be applying for it too, so anything you can do to help swing things in your favour will be a worthwhile effort. Don't worry too much. Chapter 8, 'Getting in and getting on', will help you to think more about the things you can do to enhance your career prospects.

Local newspapers

Many local newspapers advertise vacancies for computing and IT staff, usually under the heading 'Professional' or 'Technical appointments'. If you have restricted your job search to a regional area, then you will have a much better chance of finding a suitable job if you read the local papers regularly. Before you rush out and buy a copy though, check to see on which day the IT jobs are advertised. Many larger regional papers tend to have a specific day for certain types of job vacancies. For instance, the *Manchester Evening News* advertises computing and IT vacancies on a Thursday.

National newspapers

While the national daily newspapers generally advertise more computing and IT jobs than their local counterparts, these jobs are primarily aimed at graduates and those IT professionals seeking a more senior role. As you would expect, national newspapers advertise computing and IT vacancies existing throughout the UK, and in many cases they advertise jobs in other countries too. While the IT industry is continually expanding, developing new 'greenfield' sites away from the major conurbations such as Birmingham, Manchester and London, the majority of IT jobs advertised in the national papers are biased towards companies based in the London area and along the M4 'corridor'. This list should help you decide which national newspapers to read and when to read them:

Newspaper	Advertises IT jobs on
The *Guardian*	Thursday
The *Daily Telegraph*	Thursday, Saturday, Sunday
The Times	Thursday, Sunday

Specialist job-seekers' newspapers

Often published weekly, these large-format newspapers are full of jobs and careers advice and are often specific for a particular region of the UK; *Jobs North West*, for instance. While general in nature, catering for many different professions, they are categorised quite well into the separate areas. IT jobs can be found under headings such as 'Technical', 'Professional' or 'Industrial'. These newspapers are a good source of career opportunities within IT as they cater for entry at all levels in the industry, from school leavers to experienced professionals. Not only that, but they publish a large number of jobs for one particular region, often 20–30 advertisements in a single issue. It is worth spending time reading papers as soon as possible if you plan to work locally as they will highlight many of the IT skills and experience required within your area.

IT trade magazines

With an industry as diverse as IT, it is not a complete surprise to find a large number of trade magazines published specifically for the IT professional. Not all of these include appointments sections, but it is worth paying a visit to the library to have a read of them all the same. The two main general IT magazines containing job advertisements (as well as lots of other useful information, factual articles and news) are *Computing* and *Computer Weekly*. Both are well established and pride themselves on the staggering number of vacancies they publish (which at the time of writing was peaking at 87 pages of adverts!) Both of these are free to people working in the IT industry, but you can buy them at most newsagents for £1.50. There are also a number of specialist magazines worth reading which cover areas like PC hardware and software, networking, midrange and minicomputers, such as *PC Week* and *Unix Systems*.

Contact Details
Computing
VNU Business Publications, VNU House, 32–34 Broadwick Street, London W1A 2HG; 0171 316 9000

Computer Weekly
Reed Business Publishing, Quadrant House, The Quadrant, Sutton, Surrey SM2 5AS; 01444 441212

PC Week
VNU Business Publications, VNU House, 32–34 Broadwick Street, London W1A 2HG; 0171 316 9000

Network Computing
Business and Technical Communications, 24 High Street, Beckenham, Kent BR3 1AY; 0181 663 3818

Network World
LAN Circulation, Readerlink, Audit House, Field End Road, Eastcote, Ruislip, Middlesex HA4 9LT; 0181 956 3015

Unix Systems
Eaglehead Publishing, Maybury Road, Woking, Surrey GU21 5HX; 01483 740271

Accessing job vacancies on the Internet

Through the Internet you can access a huge amount of information on IT vacancies in the UK and throughout the world. In addition, you can read hundreds of helpful articles on the latest technologies, issues and general career advice. Most people access the Internet either at work, at university or at home (you can buy Internet software to run on most home PCs with a modem, through advertisements in any of the popular PC magazines).

Many companies which use IT now have a 'web site' which you can connect to if you know their address on the World Wide Web (WWW). A typical web site usually contains a 'home page' which often displays financial and recruitment information. For example, Cap Gemini, the IT services company mentioned in Chapter 3, has a web site address of: www.capgemini.co.uk

Registering with a computer recruitment agency

The current skills shortage in the IT profession is generating huge amounts of work for the specialist computer recruitment agencies, whose main role is to match their registered clients with vacancies from the various IT companies whom they represent. These agencies are extremely good at arranging a large number of interviews for their clients in a relatively short space of time – assuming they have the right skills. Agencies work on a commission basis, receiving payment from the recruiting company usually for every candidate sent for interview, plus a bonus payment should they accept the position (usually a percentage of the salary). Unfortunately, this does highlight the problem with using recruitment agencies: while they will bend over backwards to find you work if you possess suitable experience in certain key areas, they will soon lose interest in you if you cannot offer them the skills they are seeking. Many of these agencies employ highly skilled, sincere professionals, who will gladly offer career advice and guidance – but they are not a charity. Nevertheless, because of the skills shortage, many agencies are now looking for IT graduates straight from university as well as anyone with over six months' experience in the popular IT systems. Lists of computer recruitment agencies can be found in *Computing* and *Computer Weekly* or you can find them in the *Yellow Pages*, listed under 'Employment Agencies'.

Approaching employers directly

While it is all very good taking the initiative and contacting employers directly, studies have suggested this is really not worth doing unless you have 'inside knowledge' of a vacant position which has not yet been advertised. The majority of companies use specialist computer recruitment agencies to advertise positions and hold initial selection interviews on their behalf, mainly because they do not have the time to handle the hundreds of applications they would otherwise receive (many of which will be unsuitable). In one study, over 80 per cent of applicants who applied directly to the employer were politely informed there were no vacancies at the present time, but their records would be kept on file. When the employers were asked three months later about the details on their files, they admitted they did not really have time to sift through any of the applications in the file, apart from those received in response to an advertisement. If you are confident you *can* bypass this unfortunate situation, then write a short, introductory letter to the personnel manager, explaining your skills and interests, and preferably, enclosing a copy of your curriculum vitae (CV). If possible, find out the name of the Personnel Manager beforehand and address your letter accordingly – it will usually guarantee someone will read it. The following points are worth heeding when writing a speculative letter to an employer for any IT vacancy:

◆ type your letter (or use a word-processor) on good quality white A4 paper

◆ briefly describe your skills and experience (in one paragraph – the rest is on your CV)

◆ state your availability for an informal discussion or interview should they be interested

◆ leave a contact address and phone number

◆ always enclose an SAE for their reply.

Further information

Details of IT companies, including contact addresses and the computer systems they use, can be found in *The Computer Users Year Book* and *The Software Users Year Book*, usually available from the reference section of most libraries. Both are published by VNU Business Publications.

Writing a successful CV

Sooner or later, you will need to respond to a job advertisement, not only by writing a letter of application, saying why you would like the job, but also by sending a current copy of your CV. The term 'CV' literally means 'the way your life has run' and it has just one main purpose – to get you an interview with the employer. In other words, it must sell you to the employer (in about 20 seconds, because that is the average time spent reading one!). Writing a CV (and keeping it up-to-date) is something you should take very seriously, as it is often the only weapon you have in getting past the front door of many personnel departments. With this in mind, I suggest you read *Preparing Your Own CV*, published by Kogan Page, which deals with this subject superbly.

Who will employ me?

There are literally hundreds of employers who are seeking people with IT skills throughout the UK; listing them all would warrant a book in its own right! While it is easy to advise people to read the glossy magazines for names of IT companies and agencies, many people like to know the names of at least a few of the major players when they are thinking about applying for a job.

To get you started, here is a list of some of the leading IT employers in the UK; a brief introductory letter to any one of these may help you get started on your quest; all these companies participate in the British Computer Society's professional development scheme to help them plan and manage career development:

AT&T Istel Ltd, Highfield House, Headless Cross Drive, Headless Cross, Redditch, Worcs B97 5ED

Avesta Sheffield Ltd, PO Box 161, Shepcote Lane, Sheffield S9 1TR

BAA plc, Jubilee House, Furlong Way, North Terminal, Gatwick Airport,West Sussex RH6 0JN

BISS Ltd, Campus 500, Maylands Avenue, Hemel Hempstead, Herts HP2 7EE

Britannia Building Society, Head Office, PO Box 20, Newton House, Leek, Staffs, ST13 5RG

British Gas plc, Engineering Research Station, PO Box 1LH, Killingworth, Newcastle-upon-Tyne NE99 1LH

British Nuclear Fuels Ltd, CMS, Allday House, 1st Floor, Risley, Warrington, Cheshire WA3 6AS

British Rail Research, PO Box 2, London Road, Derby DE24 8YV

British Steel – Strip Products, Computer Block, Port Talbot Works, Port Talbot, West Glamorgan SA13 2NG

BT (Development and Procurement), RT9, Room 10, BT Laboratories, Martlesham Heath, Ipswich IP5 7RE

Bull Information Systems Ltd, Maxted Road, Hemel Hempstead, Herts HP2 7DZ

Cambridgeshire County Council, Department of Information Technology, Babbage House, Castle Park, Castle Hill, Cambridge CB3 0AP

CSC Computer Sciences Ltd, CSC Warton Aerodrome, Preston, Lancs PR4 1AX

Data Sciences (UK) Ltd, Pinehurst House, Farnborough, Hants GU14 7NB

Datasure Ltd, Suffolk House, 102–8 Baxter Avenue, Southend-on-Sea SS2 6JP

Defence Research Agency, Software Engineering Centre, St Andrews Road, Malvern, Worcs WR14 3PS

Department of Health, Information Systems Directorate, 302A Skipton House, 80 London Road, London SE1 6LW

The Employment Service, Information Technology Branch, Kings Court, 80 Hanover Way, Sheffield S3 7UF

Essex County Council, IT Services Division, County Hall, Chelmsford, Essex CM1 1JZ

Esso UK plc, Mail Point 06, Esso House, Ermyn Way, Leatherhead, Surrey KT22 8UX

Ford Motor Company, Ford of Europe, Finance Personnel, Central Office, Eagle Way, Brentwood, Essex CM13 3BW

GPT Ltd, Business Systems Group, Technology Drive, Beeston, Nottingham NG9 1LA

Halifax plc, 1 Lovell Park Road, Leeds LS1 1NS

HM Land Registry, Computer Services Division, Drakes Hill Court, Burrington Way, Plymouth, Devon PL5 3LP

ICI Systems, PO Box 13, The Heath, Runcorn, Cheshire WA7 4QD

International Computers Limited (ICL), Beaumont, Burfield Road, Old Windsor, Windsor, Berks SL4 2JP

Kent County Council, Policy Unit, Professional Services Department, County Hall, Maidstone, Kent ME14 1XQ

Logica UK Ltd, 68 Newman Street, London W1A 4SE

Midlands Electricity plc, Information Technology, 241 High Street, Kingswinford, West Midlands DY6 8BN

National Computing Centre, Training Division, Oxford Road, Manchester M1 7ED

National Power plc, Mistral Building, Westlea Campus, Chelmsford Road, Swindon, Wilts SN5 7EY

Northwest Water Ltd, Dawson House, Great Sankey, Warrington WA5 3LW

Post Office IT Services, Concept 2000, 250 Farnborough Road, Farnborough, Hants GU14 7LU

Royal Insurance (UK), PO Box 144, New Hall Place, Old Hall Street, Liverpool L69 3EN

The Scottish Office, IT Services, W1/13 Saughton House, Broomhouse Drive, Edinburgh EH11 3DX

Siemens Nixdorf Information Systems Ltd, The Westbrook Centre, Milton Road, Cambridge CB4 1YG

7

Getting help and training

While the graduate and A-level entry programmes of some of the larger employers is a welcome introduction to the world of computing and IT for many people, what provision is there for those of us without such qualifications? Quite a lot in fact, as there are a number of organisations which can help people find work and training within all employment areas, including IT. Here are some of the main ones you can turn to for help and advice.

◆ The Careers Service
◆ Job Centre
◆ Training and Enterprise Council
◆ Training Access Points
◆ IT Training companies
◆ Colleges and universities.

Using the Careers Service

If you are currently at school, college or university, then you will have probably been introduced to the Careers Service already. If not, then there are a number of careers offices scattered around the country who can offer the same service (you can find your nearest careers office by looking in the *Yellow Pages* under 'careers').

The Careers Service does not specialise in any one particular employment area but is fully aware of the need for skilled IT professionals within the business sector. Having links with numerous training organisations as well as IT employers, the Careers Service can provide the following services:

◆ a list of computing vacancies within the area
◆ advice on training organisations (colleges, universities and government-backed training companies) which can help you gain the necessary skills
◆ advice on studying for qualifications while in work (vocational qualifications)
◆ information on local and national employers
◆ recruitment and selection procedures, such as computer aptitude tests.

Using the Job Centre

Job Centres are situated in most towns and cities and are a prime source of help and advice for anyone seeking employment. Most people view job centres as rather depressing places that only advertise vacancies for low paid and unskilled employment opportunities. This is not the case; Job Centres regularly advertise professional and technical employment opportunities within computing and IT, mainly locally, but sometimes nationally or even internationally. For people seeking employment specifically within IT, Job Centres can provide the following services:

◆ notice of current or forthcoming IT vacancies
◆ a free Executive Recruitment Service, designed to match professional people with suitable vacancies in the IT sector
◆ a free Employment Service Programme which provides help and advice on applying for jobs, writing a CV and interview technique
◆ access to the 'Job Club' service which, if entitled, gives individuals access to a wide range of resources to help them find and apply for jobs, such as newspapers, stamps, word-processing and printing facilities
◆ advice on vocational training and other facilities offered by the Training and Enterprise Council

◆ computer-based Training Access Points (TAPs), which are easy-to-use large-scale computer screens designed to provide people with information on local training and education opportunities. Although they are for general use, there is a section on computing and IT. TAPs can also be found in many libraries

◆ leaflets, books and periodicals covering a whole range of areas, such as job vacancies, training, qualifications and employment case-studies.

The role of the Training and Enterprise Council

More commonly known as the TEC, the Training and Enterprise Council is an organisation contracted by the Department for Education and Employment to administer and coordinate a number of Youth Training Schemes throughout the UK. There are currently 82 TECs, or Local Enterprise Companies in Scotland (LECs), which operate in strict regional boundaries, based on postcode. All TECs and LECs share the same objective: to provide training opportunities for the 16+ age group. For instance, if you are a college student and you need to attend a specific IT exhibition or training seminar, the TEC can fund the cost. TECs are also key players in the Youth Credit scheme which is available to school and college leavers. Through this scheme (which might be known by another name in your area) you can access a number of training schemes, such as the Modern Apprenticeship programme, which can lead to a recognised National Vocational Qualification (NVQ) in information technology. The IT Modern Apprenticeship Scheme is now sponsored by Microsoft and an employer can send staff on IT training courses such as the Microsoft Certified Professional Engineer programme. You can find the address of your local TEC by looking in the telephone directory under 'Training'.

For more general information on training opportunities, contact: Training for Young People Division, Department for Education and Employment, Room W4d, Moorfoot, Sheffield, S1 4PQ; 0114 259 3573.

8 Getting in and getting on

for Getting into the Information Technology Industry

◆ Be able to *demonstrate* your skills or experience. Have you written a program either at home or in college which you can mention in an interview? Have you diagnosed a problem with a friend's computer and subsequently fixed it? Any practical experience is worth its weight in gold.

◆ Talk to the employers. They need staff as much as you need a job. Ask the personnel or human resources manager what skills or qualifications they expect potential employees to possess. Showing initiative often creates opportunity.

◆ Many employers now want IT staff to have a broad understanding of *all* the issues affecting IT, not just an understanding of one particular area. Reading the IT trade magazines will help boost your knowledge. Understanding IT generally will also prepare you for any tricky questions you might get asked in an interview situation, such as 'Where do you think the IT industry is going in terms of desktop computing?'

◆ Be flexible and open-minded. Seek opportunity. If you are offered a job in IT which is not the one you hoped for, it might be worth taking it to gain experience. See if you can transfer between teams at a later stage or go on a suitable training course.

◆ Remember the skills shortage. Try and identify an area where you could fit in quickly; determine what skills you need and aim to satisfy them.

◆ Be patient – the IT industry will still be here tomorrow. If you need to do a three-year degree course to achieve your career goals, do it.

◆ Get as much hands-on experience as you can. PCs are commonplace now – try and get hold of one if possible and teach yourself the basic skills. Try and give yourself a sensible project to complete, which will expose you to the main areas you need to be familiar with. Many of the skills which will be in demand are PC-based which can be learnt at home, such as Visual Basic, C++ and Microsoft Office.

◆ The IT revolution has created a huge selection of associated teach-yourself books, videos and manuals, many of which are used every day within the IT industry. If you don't want to buy them, visit the library and check out the computing section.

9

The future of computing and information technology

Considering the current rate of change, it would take a brave soul to predict exactly what will happen to the IT industry within the next three years, let alone the next ten years. There is one event, however, which will affect the whole of the IT industry on a massive scale, and that is the arrival of the year 2000. Of course, there is nothing unique about the year 2000 itself: it is the way it will be represented in a computer that is causing concern throughout the industry.

Currently, most computer programs store only the last two characters of the year, as in '96' or '97', which at the moment is fine. However, come the year 2000, following the same rules, the same field will now contain '00', which, as you might guess, is going to cause a lot of problems to a great many users of computing and information technology throughout the world.

As a result of the warnings issued by the government and all of the top IT consultancies, many companies have now started major recruitment drives covering all the major technical areas of business computing. Their objectives are simple – to build project teams to help identify the impact of this change on their organisation and to make sure that all their computer systems become 'year 2000-compliant' before it is too late.

Not surprisingly, industry watchdogs have predicted a huge rise in the number of programmers working within IT in the years up to the year 2000, especially those with COBOL experience, this being the language thousands (if not millions) of business applications have been written in all over the world.

It is predicted that even by the year 2000, there will *still* be a severe skills shortage in IT. While demand for core IT skills remains high, there will be an even greater need for people with skills relating to PC and UNIX systems development, relational database systems, LAN development and, probably most importantly, Internet development.

The growth of the Internet into a world-wide business application is still a few years away, but even now all the major IT software suppliers are providing systems which will enable the Internet to be used for commercial business applications, such as electronic retailing.

Marketing on the Internet is now also playing an increasingly important role in electronic commerce, and forecasts for the year 2000 estimate sales in this new area to be $70–$200 billion worldwide. Already, some of the major banks in the UK offer on-line banking services over a private network. One report published in 1995 on the growth of 'on-line' services predicted 80 per cent of European banks will offer a full banking service over the Internet within three years. Another survey suggested that PC banking in Europe will be used by more than 7.8 million retail banking users by the year 2001.

Such widespread growth in the Internet (it is estimated that there will be between 200 and 500 million Internet users in five years' time), means there is huge demand for the programming languages and applications used to develop these new Internet services. Even now, the IT industry is crying out for skills such as UNIX, C++, Java and HTML (a language used to develop 'web' applications) to help satisfy this demand.

The future of computing and information technology does not, however, rest solely with the development of global networking. With increases in the sheer processing capability of even the average PC, combined with new developments in software engineering fields, computer applications such as 'virtual reality' are now increasing in popularity. These sophisticated computer systems allow the user to see images of physical objects and locations as though they were actually there. Soon, it will be possible to go to your favourite holiday destination and see the sights just by visiting your local travel agent!

Without doubt, there are many challenges facing the IT industry over the next five years but, equally, many opportunities to embrace new technologies. IT already has made a significant impact on society, and the future will be no different. If this book has but one objective, it is to help you become part of that future.

10 Qualifications available

While many computing careers have been built around experience alone, there a number of good reasons for obtaining an IT-related qualification:

- meeting membership criteria for professional IT bodies such as the British Computer Society
- to gain accelerated promotion into management positions
- as a 'passport' for moving between IT jobs throughout the country.

Of course, professional qualifications on their own do not guarantee success – training and experience are also needed in many areas – but there is no doubt that a computing qualification indicates to a potential employer your level of commitment and intellectual capability, and provides a foundation for future career development.

As well as gaining academic skills, courses such as degrees and higher diplomas can also provide you with many of the 'soft' skills which are highly sought after in industry, such as team-working and project management.

Business and Technology Education Council (BTEC) Certificates and Diplomas

BTEC qualifications are recognised nationally in England, Wales and Northern Ireland and in some countries overseas and are run in schools, colleges, universities and through many companies.

BTEC courses, being vocational in nature, tend to offer practical computing skills rather than academic theory and are widely respected for their relevance to computing occupations within the industry. Being seen as equivalent to A-levels, many BTEC qualifications are also accepted by universities for entry to a degree programme. In Scotland, the role of BTEC is performed by the Scottish Vocational Educational Council (SCOTVEC).

The main qualifications BTEC provide for careers in computing and IT are:

◆ First Certificate/Diploma – age on entry 16+, one year, equivalent to two GCSEs at grades A–C.★ For entry to A-levels, BTEC National qualification and NVQ Level 3
◆ Advanced GNVQ (General NVQ) – no formal entry requirements, normally two years, but no real time constraints, equivalent to two A-levels★
◆ National Certificate/Diploma – no formal entry requirements, three years part-time/two-years full-time, equivalent to two A-levels★
◆ Higher National Certificate/Diploma – no formal entry requirements, but any of the following would indicate suitability: one A-level, BTEC National qualification, equivalent to a degree★
◆ NVQ Levels 3, 4 and 5.

★ Due to the vocational nature of BTEC programmes, a direct comparison is not always appropriate. These are the generally accepted equivalents.

University degrees

There is now a wide variety of computing degrees available from universities which go some way beyond the 'standard' computer science degree, reflecting the importance the industry is placing on new technologies. For example, courses such as Artificial Intelligence, Systems Analysis and Software Engineering are now readily available, which will help you enter more specialised fields of employment within the IT industry.

The most common route through university is an honours degree or an ordinary degree, which in England, Wales and Northern Ireland is three years' full-time study, or four years in length, including a year's placement in industry (a 'sandwich' course). Remembering that employers are looking for practical skills as well as academic knowledge, a year spent in industry will always attract the attention of many personnel managers, and can often mean a larger starting salary in some cases.

While entry to higher education can be achieved through courses such as BTEC National Certificates and Diplomas, the most popular route to university is by taking A-levels. With one or two A-levels, you can usually apply for an ordinary degree, but for honours degrees, three A-levels are normally expected. You do not need mathematics or computing A-levels, but you do need to get the highest grades you can as competition for degrees in computing and information technology is fierce. If, however, you decide to study for a scientific degree, such as software engineering or computational mathematics, you will normally be expected to have good A-level grades in mathematics. Similarly, for a degree in a subject with an electronic bias, you will need A-levels in either mathematics, physics or electronics.

National Vocational Qualifications

National Vocational Qualifications (NVQs or S/NVQs in Scotland) in computing and information technology are a new and flourishing framework of nationally recognised awards which have been jointly developed by the IT profession and the Information Technology Industry Training Association (ITITO). The main aim of an IT NVQ is to provide people with skills which are used and recognised by the IT industry, by adopting a more practical approach to training. Each award is made up of a series of work units which relate to the NVQ topic; the number of units studied is dependent upon the level of NVQ. There are five levels of NVQ:

◆ Level 1 provides basic skills, roughly equivalent to GCSEs.

◆ Level 2 builds on skills and develops greater understanding.
◆ Level 3 assumes more responsibility in the role (equivalent to A-levels).
◆ Levels 4 and 5 provide a professional and postgraduate level of understanding.

Why should I consider an NVQ?

◆ Not everyone is comfortable sitting exams. NVQs assess your competence at work and rarely involve exams.
◆ They relate to the real word – a real advantage.
◆ NVQs are flexible. There are no time limits, no age limits and no special entry requirements.

NVQs in computing and information technology are offered by many colleges and training institutions throughout the UK and are awarded by a number of examinations bodies which all offer their own IT NVQ. For example, the following NVQs are awarded by the City & Guilds of London Institute:

◆ Using Information Technology
◆ Use and Support of Information Technology
◆ Operating Information Technology
◆ Software Creation
◆ Installing Information Technology Products
◆ Supporting Users of Information Technology
◆ Information Systems Analysis
◆ Information Systems Design and Programming
◆ Implementing Information Technology Solution.

For more information on the NVQ framework, contact: an IT employer (they might operate an NVQ scheme); your local college of further education; the Job Centre or the Training and Enterprise Council (TEC).

Alternatively, contact:
The National Council for Vocational Qualifications (NCVQ), Customer Services, NCVQ, 222 Euston Road, London, NW1 2BZ; 0171 728 1914

City & Guilds Basic Certificate in Computer Programming

The City & Guilds (C&G) Institute awards a number of qualifications which are widely recognised and appreciated by IT employers. The C&G certificate in computer programming is a popular choice for many people who want to enter the IT profession directly (or straight from school) as a trainee or junior programmer. Most of the courses offered by the C&G Institute require no formal entry qualifications, although it is better if you do possess O-level English language and mathematics or the equivalent.

Royal Society of Arts qualifications

Founded in 1754, the Royal Society of Arts (RSA) provides a number of qualifications covering IT in general as well as specific IT applications. RSA programmes are offered by approved centres which can be training institutions or colleges of further education. The main RSA qualifications include:

◆ Computer Literacy and Information Technology (CLAIT). A popular, flexible course in IT which is taken annually by 120,000+ candidates, 40 per cent of whom are school children. CLAIT is an employable qualification in its own right, but also provides a solid grounding for further study, such as GNVQ, NVQ or A-level.
◆ Integrated Business Technology Stage II. A more advanced course integrating a number of IT applications in a simulated office situation, requiring some knowledge of hardware. To enrol, you will need skills at least to CLAIT level.

Vendor-specific qualifications

In the pursuit of gaining highly productive staff very quickly, some employers now prefer applicants with specific qualifications in IT software and hardware as opposed to the more generic IT qualifications available in colleges and universities. Vendor-specific qualifications are now becoming as important as degrees and diplomas with many companies as they certify competency in a product which is recognised throughout the world.

Leading vendor-specific qualifications

◆ Certified Novell Administrator (CNA) – to handle day-to-day administration of an installed Novell networking product, such as Netware4 or Netware3.

◆ Certified Novell Engineer (CNE) – installing and upgrading network systems and performing tuning

◆ Microsoft Certified Product Specialist (MCPS) – qualified to install, configure and support Microsoft desktop products. MCPSs have considerable knowledge in one of the Microsoft operating systems.

◆ Microsoft Certified Systems Engineer (MCSE) – qualified to install and support Windows NT and server products. Candidates must pass a total of six exams to achieve certification.

◆ Certified Java Programmer – gaining knowledge in basic Java programming techniques.

◆ Certified Java Developer – more in-depth knowledge of Java, including memory management, screen design and graphics. To gain this qualification you must first possess the Certified Java Programmer qualification.

Where to study

University courses

For details of all university courses and entrance requirements, consult the University and Colleges Admissions Service (UCAS) Handbook.

For all matters concerning university admission and student loans, contact:

UCAS, Fulton House, Jessop Avenue, Cheltenham, Gloucestershire, GL50 3SH; 01242 227788

Open University Degrees

The Open University (OU) specialises in offering a wide range of courses (including degrees) which are completed at home. To obtain an OU degree, you need to accumulate credits in core and supplementary modules over a number of years. For more information on the Open University, contact:

The Open University, Central Enquiry Service, PO Box 200, Walton Hall, Milton Keynes, MK7 6YZ; 01908 653231

College courses

Many colleges now offer good full-time, part-time or evening classes which are often cheap and sometimes free. For details of colleges offering A-levels, C&G/RSA awards, GNVQs, NVQs and BTECs, use a TAP, visit your TEC or read *CRAC Directory of Further Education*, published by Hobsons Publishing, available in the reference section of most libraries.

City & Guilds of London Institute Examinations

For details of examinations and approved study centres, contact:

City & Guilds of London Institute, 1 Giltspur Street, London, EC1A 9DD; 0171 294 2468

National Vocational Qualifications

For details of colleges and training establishments offering NVQs in IT you must first contact one of the NVQ awarding bodies. All of the following organisations award NVQs in IT and can provide details of courses and places to study:

British Computer Society, 1 Sandford Street, Swindon, SN1 1HJ; 01793 417147

City & Guilds of London Institute, 1 Giltspur Street, London, EC1A 9DD; 0171 294 2468

National Computing Centre, Oxford House, Oxford Road, Manchester, M1 7ED; 0161 228 6333

RSA Examinations Board, Westwood Way, Coventry, CV4 8HS; 01203 470033

Business and Technology Education Council, c/o Edexcel Foundation, Stewart House, 32 Russell Square, London WC1B 5DN; 0171 393 4444

London Chamber of Commerce and Industry (LCCI), Marlow House, Station Road, Sidcup, Kent, DA5 7BJ 0181 302 0261

Telecommunications Vocational Standards Council, Blackfriars House, 339 South Row, Central Milton Keynes, MK9 2PG; 01908 20120

Pitman Examinations Institute, 1 Giltspur Street, London, EC1A 9DD; 0171 294 2471

SCOTVEC, Hanover House, 24 Douglas Street, Glasgow, G2 7NQ; 0141 248 7900

City & Guilds Scotland, 22 Walker Street, Edinburgh, EH3 7HR; 0131 226 1556

National Computing Centre Scotland, Anderson House, 389 Argyle Street, Glasgow, G2 8LF; 0141 2043725

Major IT training companies

All of the major computing and IT vendors run in-house courses, covering a wide range of topics on many different platforms. As you would expect, the standard of the tuition is extremely high and, as many courses provide 'hands-on' experience in the class-room, these courses are very popular among IT professionals. As an individual, before you attend one of these courses you should think very seriously about cost – they are not cheap and you may find a similar course, costing considerably less, being run at a local college.

Commercial training companies – and what they provide

Sun Educational Services, Sun Service Division, Sun Microsystems Ltd., Watchmoor Park, Riverside Way, Camberley, Surrey, GU15 3YL; 01276 416520

Courses: UNIX programming, networking, client-server connectivity, application design, relational database management, Java programming and certification.

Amdahl UK Education, Beaumont, Old Windsor, Berkshire, SL4 2JP; 01753 833555

Courses: management skills, service management – help desk, disaster recovery; personal skills – presentation skills, communication skills; networking; LANs; Novell netware; UNIX and AIX;

mainframe systems programming; systems analysis and design; database programming.

IBM Education; 0345 581329

Courses: mainframe computing; AS/400; UNIX (AIX); OS/2; PC; Windows NT; Novell netware; networking; application development; Lotus programming; database programming.

Learning Tree International, Mole Business Park, Leatherhead, Surrey, KT22 7AD; 01372 364610 or 0800 282353

Courses: SAP R/3; Microsoft courses (inc. MCSE); networking; netware (inc. CNE/CNA), Internet/Intranet; PC support; UNIX, OS/2, C/C++; database programming; software development; management skills.

Novell UK Education and Training. For all Novell courses, including CNA and CNE certification, tel: 0800 966196.

Oracle Education. For training on all Oracle products and general IT skills, tel: 0345 777711.

Microsoft Education. For training in all Microsoft products and MCPS/MCSE certification. Microsoft has a large number of approved training centres where you can obtain training throughout the UK. Contact: **Microsoft Limited**, Microsoft Place, Winnersh, Wokingham, Berkshire, RG41 5TP; Training hotline: 0345 000111

12 Useful addresses

IT professional bodies

The following professional organisations figure significantly in the development of IT in the UK and are a prime source of information regarding career development and training.

The British Computer Society (BCS) 1 Sandford Street, Swindon, SN1 1HJ; 01793 417417

The Council of European Professional Informatics Societies (CEPIS), 7 Mansfield Mews, London, W1M 9FJ; 0171 637 5607

The Engineering Council, 10 Maltravers Street, London, WC2R 3ER; 0171 240 7891

The Institute of Data Processing Management (IDPM), IDPM House, Edgington Way, Ruxley Corner, Sidcup, Kent, DA14 5HR; 0181 308 0747

The Association of Computer Professionals, 240 Barnett Wood Lane, Ashtead, Surrey, KT21 2DB; 0372 273442

Education and IT

National Information and Learning Technologies Association (NILTA), c/o Leeds College of Building, North Street, Leeds, LS2 7QT; 01332 2343598

NILTA provide assistance on the use and development of IT in colleges of further education

Information on Grants and Loans for students

Student Loans Company Limited, 100 Bothwell Street, Glasgow, G2 7JD; 0800 405 0100

Department for Education and Employment, Publications Centre, PO Box 6927, London, E3 3NZ; 0171 510 0150

13 Further reading

Job hunting

Corfield, R *Successful Interview Skills*, Kogan Page
Byron, M *How To Pass Graduate Recruitment Tests*, Kogan Page
Modha, S *How To Pass Computer Selection Tests*, Kogan Page

Teaching

Taylor, F *Careers in Teaching*, Kogan Page

Education and qualifications

British Qualifications, Kogan Page
British Vocational Qualifications, Kogan Page
Sponsorship for Students published and distributed by the Careers
  Research Advisory Centre (CRAC) and Hobsons Publishing.
  Contains 2,500 scholarships and bursaries from 200 different
  organisations. Copies are available at £7.95 from Customer
  Services REF F30, Biblios PDS Ltd, Star Road, Partridge
  Green, West Sussex, RH13 8LD; 01403 710851.

Employment opportunities

Freelance Year Book; *Considering Computer Contracting*; *Getting Com-*

puter Jobs Abroad; all published by Computer Weekly Publications, PO Box 935, Finchingfield, Braintree, Essex, CM7 4LN; 0371 811160.

Useful books on computing and IT

General

Carter, L and Huzan, E *Teach Yourself Computers and Their Use*, Hodder Headline

PC

Rathbone, A *Upgrading and Fixing PCs for Dummies*, IDG Books
Aspinwall, J and Todd, M *Troubleshooting Your PC*, MIS Press
Kraynak, J *Complete Idiot's Guide to PCs*, Que
Press, B *PC Upgrade and Repair Bible*, IDG Books

The Internet

Tretter, M *How To Use The Internet*, ZD Press
Crumlish, C *The ABCs of the Internet*, Sybex
Bride, M *Teach Yourself the Internet*, Hodder & Stoughton

Popular operating systems

McMullen, J *The Complete Idiot's Guide to UNIX,* Alpha Books
Levine, J and Young, M *Unix for Dummies*, IDG Books
Joy, M *Beginning Unix*, ITP
Crawford, S *The ABCs of Windows 95*, Sybex
Kotecha, H *Windows 95 in Easy Steps*, Computer Step
Kotecha, H *Windows for Workgroups 3.11 in Easy Steps*, Computer Step
Weixel, S *Using Windows 3.11*, Que
Rathbone, A *Windows for Dummies*, IDG Books

Programming languages

Liberty, J *Teach Yourself C++ Programming in 21 Days*, Sams
    Publishing
Gookin, D *C for Dummies*, IDG Books
Wilks, I *Instant C++ Programming*, WROX
Kesler, G *The Beginners Guide to C*, WROX
Davis, S R *C++ for Dummies*, IDG Books

Oracle database software

Oracle: The Complete Reference; *Oracle: A Beginner's Guide*; *Oracle:
    Developer/2000 Handbook*; *PL/SQL Programming*; *Oracle DBA
    Handbook*; all published by Osborne/McGraw-Hill (also
    available from Oracle; tel 0990 997788 and ask for the
    bookshop).

Networking

Sheldon, T *Netware 4.1: The Complete Reference*,
    Osborne/McGraw-Hill
Jordan, L and Churchill, B *Communications and Networking for the
    PC*, New Riders Publishing

Systems development methodologies

Weaver, P L *Practical SSADM Version 4*, Pitman Publishing

Computer training videos and software

Many libraries now stock computer training videos, covering subjects such as Microsoft Office, Wordperfect, Pascal and DBase IV.

A good selection of videos covering subjects such as UNIX,
C++, Windows 95 and Visual Basic is available from The Software Warehouse, The Gyratory, Hangar Lane, London W5 1EE;
0181 810 7770 or 01675 466 467

A larger selection of about 200 titles, including subjects such as
the Internet, OS/2 and netware administration, is available from

Burgess Video Group, Unit 18, Industrial Estate, Brecon, Powys LD3 8LA; 01874 611633. This company also supplies computer-based training software on CD-ROM for use on IBM-compatible PCs with a CD-ROM drive. There are over 200 CD-ROM titles in stock covering many Microsoft products, C/C++ programming, Windows 95 and the Internet.

Glossary

Artificial Intelligence (AI)   computer systems which perform human functions which would normally require intelligence, eg reasoning and decision-making.

Assembler   a programming language which is used to code information which will then be converted into machine code.

AS/400   IBM midrange computer.

Bar code   information stored as a series of printed stripes. Often found on food and clothes labels.

Bridge   a device that connects two networks together.

C   a high-level programming language originally developed for use with the UNIX operating system.

C++   a more advanced version of the C programming language.

CD-ROM   Compact Disc–Read Only Memory. A small plastic disc that is used as a high capacity storage device. A CD-ROM player is the device that enables a computer to read the CD-ROM.

Client-server architecture   a network of computers in which a central (server) computer carries out tasks in response to instructions from other computers (clients) in the network.

COBOL   Common Ordinary Business-Oriented Language. A programming language used extensively for writing business applications.

Console   a computer terminal which allows a computer operator to access the computer system, usually in order to issue operating system commands.

CPU   Central Processing Unit. A group of circuits that perform the basic functions of the computer.

Database   a collection of files stored in a structured way, that can be accessed by many users from computer terminals.

Distributed computing   computer systems using more than one processor in different locations, all connected to a central computer.

Ethernet   a local area network protocol (a set of rules which determine how data should be transmitted and received across a LAN).

Expert system   software that applies the knowledge of a human expert in a particular field to help diagnose problems.

Gateway   a device used to link two different types of networks together, eg a LAN and a WAN.

High-level language   a programming language that is usually easy to learn, allowing the programmer to write programs using English-like statements. A separate operation is then performed to translate this code into instructions the computer will understand.

HTML   Hypertext Markup Language - a programming language used to develop Internet applications.

Interactive   a system or piece of software that allows conversation to take place between the user and the computer system, for example a computer game being controlled by a joystick is deemed interactive.

Internet   an international wide area network connecting together many local networks that provides electronic mail and file transfer facilities.

Intranet   a term given to a local or secure Internet, eg an Internet which exists within one company for use by its employees.

Jackson Structured Programming (JSP)   a popular method of writing and designing structured computer programs, developed by Michael Jackson.

Java   a high level computer programming language developed for writing interactive Internet applications.

LAN   Local Area Network. A system of computer terminals and devices connected together within a short distance of each other eg, a series of PCs linked together in the IT department of an organisation.

Microchip   an electronic circuit used in the assembly of microcomputers etched onto a silicon semiconductor (or 'chip').

Modem   a device that allows computer data to be transmitted over telephone lines.

Monitor   a visual display unit (VDU) used to display high quality text and graphics on a computer.

MVS   Multiple Virtual Storage. A popular IBM mainframe operating system.

Online   connected to and under the control of a computer.

Online banking   accessing banking services, usually over a network, via a computer.

Operating system   a series of programs that control the basic functions of a computer system, such as input/output, memory allocation and file-handling.

PC   personal computer. A general term relating to a microcomputer having an Intel processor based on the IBM PC style architecture.

Psuedo-code   English-like sentences which are used in program design to describe the operation of the program.

Real-time   a computer system that processes events as they happen, allowing decisions to be made that could influence those events.

Router   a communications device that accepts data and forwards it onto its destination using the most efficient route through the network.

Server   a computer on a network that provides services used by other computers in the network.

Software engineering – a computing field covering all aspects of software development.

SSADM   a popular systems development methodology.

Terminal   a device consisting of a visul display unit and a keyboard that provides access to a computer system.

Token ring   a popular type of LAN architecture in which a computer connected to it can only transmit data when it is in possession of a token.

Transaction   a general term usually relating to any single action that affects a database system eg, adding a new user to the payroll system.

UNIX   a popular multi-user operating system developed by AT&T Bell Laboratories that runs on almost any computer, from a PC to a mainframe.

Virus   a program which attaches to a computer system and then spreads itself to other files or computers on the network, often corrupting them in the process.

Visual Basic   a popular PC-based programming language.

WAN   a network that connects computers over large distances using high-speed telephone lines, radio and satellites.

Windows   an extremely popular GUI developed by Microsoft Corporation, allowing complex tasks to be performed by clicking icons on the screen with a mouse.

X25   a popular communications protocol used on WANs.

Index

Index